Powerlifting

Barney Groves

Human Kinetics

Library of Congress Cataloging-in-Publication Data

Groves, Barney R., 1936-
     Powerlifting / Barney Groves.
          p.   cm.
     Includes index.
     ISBN 0-88011-978-0
          1. Weight lifting.   I. Title.
     GV546.3.G76   2000
     613.7'13--dc21   00-024484

ISBN-10: 0-88011-978-0

ISBN-13: 978-0-88011-978-8

Copyright © 2000 by Barney Groves

Acquisitions Editor: Martin Barnard; **Managing Editor:** Leigh LaHood; **Copyeditor:** Jan Feeney; **Proofreader:** Joanna Hatzopoulos; **Indexer:** Betty Frizzéll; **Graphic Designer:** Nancy Rasmus; **Graphic Artist:** Sandra Meier; **Cover Designer:** Kristin King; **Photographer (cover):** Tom Roberts; **Photographer (interior):** photo on page 139 © Greg Simmons, all other photos by Tom Roberts; **Printer:** United Graphics

Human Kinetics books are available at special discounts for bulk purchase. Special editions or book excerpts can also be created to specification. For details, contact the Special Sales Manager at Human Kinetics.

Printed in the United States of America   10   9   8   7   6   5   4

Human Kinetics
Web site: www.HumanKinetics.com

United States: Human Kinetics, P.O. Box 5076, Champaign, IL 61825-5076
800-747-4457
e-mail: humank@hkusa.com

Canada: Human Kinetics, 475 Devonshire Road, Unit 100, Windsor, ON N8Y 2L5
800-465-7301 (in Canada only)
e-mail: orders@hkcanada.com

Europe: Human Kinetics, 107 Bradford Road, Stanningley
Leeds LS28 6AT, United Kingdom
+44 (0) 113 255 5665
e-mail: hk@hkeurope.com

Australia: Human Kinetics, 57A Price Avenue, Lower Mitcham, South Australia 5062
08 8372 0999
e-mail: liaw@hkaustralia.com

New Zealand: Human Kinetics, Division of Sports Distributors NZ Ltd.
P.O. Box 300 226 Albany, North Shore City, Auckland
0064 9 448 1207
e-mail: info@humankinetics.co.nz

To all the people
who spend countless hours
practicing and promoting
the sport of powerlifting.

Contents

Acknowledgments

This book would never have been completed without the encouragement and help of the following people. I would like to thank Rich Coppins, Barbara Beasley, Kent Johnson, Dave Weiss, Kathy Roberts, Gigi Leader, and Mike Craven. I also give special thanks to Rolfe Engels, who convinced me to compete the first time.

Introduction

If you are a powerlifter or an intermediate- to advanced-level strength trainer who wants to pursue powerlifting, this book provides a comprehensive guide to the process. You may want to pursue powerlifting for any of these reasons:

- You have experimented with the three powerlifts and are considering competing.

- You have already competed in a meet and want to improve your program of training and nutrition.

- You are a strength trainer who is competing in a sport (e.g., football) that requires a great deal of total body strength.

This guide is especially useful for lifters who are in the early stages of powerlifting programs and need guidance about what really works, as proven by the most well-known and successful powerlifters. You will be guided through

- the scientific principles of building power and strength,

- the benefits of participating in powerlifting,

- selection of the proper facility and equipment,

- use of the proper supplements,

- the most effective and legal lifting aids,

- the proper nutrition for training,

- the various training routines and a training cycle,

- the best preparation for a meet,

- determining your most successful body weight,

- proper lifting techniques and support exercises,

- a meet strategy, and

- "psyching up" for a meet or training session.

Whether you are just starting out in the sport of powerlifting or have been participating in the sport for many years, I hope this book will provide an enjoyable and rewarding experience.

Building Power and Strength

The term *powerlifting* means different things to different people. The average person will immediately think of big people and heavy weights, and someone who knows nothing about the sport will think of *Olympic lifting* due to the exposure it has received on television during the Olympic Games. Those who are familiar with the sport of powerlifting are aware that Olympic lifting and powerlifting are completely different and require different training techniques. Olympic lifting is a two-lift sport—*snatch*, and *clean and jerk*—requiring speed, strength, and technique. Powerlifting is a three-lift sport—*squat, bench press*, and *deadlift*—requiring strength and technique but no time constraint or speed.

In powerlifting terms, *power* means movement of weight in a short period of time. This movement includes one's own body weight. *Strength* means the maximum force that a muscle or muscle group can generate to move a load through a full range of motion during one repetition. This is commonly expressed as the *one repetition maximum*, or *1RM*. The term *strength lifting* is a more appropriate name for the sport of powerlifting because strength does not have a time factor. However, the term *power-lifting* is firmly associated with the squat, bench press, and deadlift competition, so from this point on, the terms *power* and *strength* will be used interchangeably.

Factors Affecting Power and Strength Gains

There are many myths and confusion surrounding the meaning of strength, the fastest and easiest way to gain both muscle mass and strength, and how to determine the difference between a good program and a bad one. The first thing to remember is that strength is not easy to develop and that you cannot gain strength in a short period of time. A valuable commodity such as strength comes slowly and must be achieved with dedication and patience. There is no easy way to do this that is also safe. Strength is the foundation on which we build other things, such as muscular endurance, power, coordination, and proper technique. Many of my colleagues think that strength is not the foundation—it is only one of the factors of physical fitness and sport skill. I base my argument on the following facts:

1. Strength is the ability to lift something once; muscular endurance is the ability to lift that weight many times, but you must first be able to do it the first time.

2. Power is strength in the shortest period of time. An example of this is moving your own weight quickly. If your legs and hips are very strong, it is easy to move your body weight quickly, but if your legs and hips are weak, it is difficult, or impossible, to move quickly.

3. Coordination and proper technique are developed only after adequate strength is gained. You can concentrate on proper technique if the weight is easy to handle. For example, if you are shooting a basketball from a distance and you can barely get the ball to the basket, you will not be able to aim for the small opening of the goal. Remember that if strength development were as easy as some people think, everyone would be strong.

Neural Changes

When you began to train with weights you were probably excited at how fast you improved at first, but the quick gains began to taper off and improvements began to come much more slowly. The initial rapid improvement is known as *neural change*, which is also commonly known as *coordination*. Remember your first attempts at bench pressing and how the weight wobbled all over the area above your chest, and when you lowered the bar it never touched your chest in the same place twice? Your body was trying to do what you wanted but did not know which muscles were necessary to perform the move. Therefore, the muscles of the arms, chest, deltoids, and upper back were all trying to help out but were actually interfering with, or working against, the muscles that were necessary to do the lift. However, in a short period of time you became steady and consistent with the movement, and the amount of weight you were lifting increased dramatically. Your body learned which muscles were necessary to perform certain lifts and which muscles were not involved. Neural and coordination improvement can only be developed by repeating the exercise many times using proper form and technique. Coordination not only makes it a more efficient task, allowing you to lift more, but also conserves energy needed for additional training. This period of neural changes is also the time you are developing proper lifting techniques, increasing your lifting ability, and decreasing the possibility of injury. Proper technique will be discussed in more detail when the exercises are presented in chapter 8.

Gains in Muscle Mass

The factors that determine increased muscle mass, or size, and increased strength and power are not fully understood. However, factors that are often discussed and generally accepted by physiologists and researchers are hypertrophy, hyperplasia, and genetic potential.

Hypertrophy

Scientists have believed and taught that people are born with a certain number of muscle fibers and this number cannot be increased. This means that you must increase the size of the existing fibers to become larger and stronger. Very thin protein, myofibril (actin and myosin), within the fibers increases in size as a result of strength training, and the protein builds a larger fiber, which produces bigger muscles and greater strength. This increase in the size of the existing muscle fiber is called *hypertrophy*.

Hyperplasia

Hyperplasia is defined as the increase in size caused by an increase in the number of muscle fibers. This is believed to occur as a result of a very intense long-term exercise program causing the involved fibers to split lengthwise and form additional fibers. The increase in number of muscle fibers has been observed in elite bodybuilders and powerlifters who have trained intensely for years. Researchers are still investigating this idea, but due to the painful process involved in obtaining muscle fiber samples, limited research has been performed involving human subjects. The process of obtaining muscle fiber samples involves cutting a small piece of muscle fiber from the center of the muscle. The subject then participates in a strenuous training program, and again another sample of fiber is cut from the same muscle. The two muscle fiber samples are then compared.

You might be asking the question, "Does the training program change if I am trying to increase fiber size or number?" The answer is no. The training programs necessary to develop either hypertrophy or hyperplasia are the same.

Genetic Potential

If we accept hypertrophy as the main process causing fibers to increase in size, then we must also accept the idea of genetic limitations regarding the extent to which muscle will increase in size. Just as we know that some people are born with muscle-tendon attachments favoring force development, the same is true in regard to the number of muscle fibers. Some people are born with a greater number of muscle fibers than others, and therefore their genetic potential for muscle size, strength, and power is greater. Some people will take this information and use it as an excuse for giving up when their improvement is slow or stops altogether. However, this is not a reasonable excuse for giving up, because anyone who truly develops what they have to the fullest extent will be successful. Your challenge is to eliminate negative thoughts and design an effective program of training that is best for you and to train with a realistic goal in mind so that you will develop your full potential.

Muscle Changes as a Result of Resistance Training

The human body is *not* a machine. A machine constructed of metal, plastic, or rubber wears out from use. Parts must be replaced periodically even if you don't misuse the machine. A machine will not improve with use, especially if you push the machine past its normal operating capacity. The harder and more often you use it, the faster it wears out. However, this is not true with the human body. The body not only responds best when used but improves when it is pushed past what it is normally accustomed to doing. When the muscles are overloaded, the body responds by making the muscles larger and stronger in that area. If you continue to overload, the muscles will continue to improve, which is the philosophy behind resistance training for added strength. Remember how it feels after an intense training session when the muscles burn? Two days later the muscles are very sore and you wonder if this should happen. Yes, this should happen if you are training intensely enough to increase the size of your muscles. The soreness you feel is the tearing down and rebuilding process, which produces bigger and stronger muscles each time they are torn down and rebuilt. You will quickly learn to associate the discomfort with a positive feeling of a good workout and a productive training session. As you associate more and more with people who are dedicated to becoming stronger, you will hear many times, "I am so sore I can hardly move." This can be considered a way to brag about a good training session. However, the nonlifters among us will think you are a little crazy if they hear you bragging about how great it is to be sore.

Selecting a Training Facility

Selecting the proper training facility can mean the difference between success and failure in your powerlifting program. There are several things to consider before joining a club, such as quality and types of equipment, location, time, atmosphere, cost, and availability of training partners.

Equipment. Does the club have the proper equipment for a powerlifting program, and is enough equipment available? Take a quick inventory to determine if the following items are offered:

- Several Olympic power bars that can withstand weights over 1,000 pounds

- Two or more safety squat racks

- Various sizes of Olympic weight plates totaling at least 2,000 pounds

- Locks of various sizes to secure the plates while lifting

- Bench press benches sturdy enough to support 800 pounds

- Chalk to use for maintaining a good grip

Location. How far do you have to drive for your workout? Pick the club closest to where you live or work if it meets all other criteria for a good training program.

Time. Even the most dedicated lifters usually have a full-time job, a family, and other obligations, making the time necessary to get a proper workout very important. Make sure that you do not have to spend valuable time waiting for equipment. Also take into account a club's hours of operation; make sure it is open when you are available to work out.

Atmosphere. Is the facility set up for powerlifting, or is it a fitness center that really prefers not to cater to powerlifters? There has to be a special area for powerlifters because of the safety factor. The area should be set apart from other areas, and it should have a specially constructed floor, in case the weights are dropped, to protect against structural damage to the building.

Cost. Cost of membership at a club can vary greatly depending on where you live. The range will be from $400 to $1,000 per year. Extra luxuries, such as steam, sauna, whirlpools, and massages, will drive the prices up and they are not necessary for a good training program. However, if you have the money to spare, treat yourself—you deserve it.

Training partners. Perhaps the most important requirement is a facility where other powerlifters regularly work out. This is a sport where the participants need encouragement from others. When you train to your maximum each session you will have your off days, and the urge to quit will happen often. Encouragement from experienced powerlifting friends who have worked through the same difficulties can mean the difference between quitting and continuing to train.

Learning Proper Spotting and Safety Techniques

Safety in the weight room is a must. When you have hundreds of pounds on your back or over your face, throat, and chest, you want to be certain that all people involved are trained in the proper spotting and safety techniques. When a person spots you in a bench press with your maximum weight, you are literally putting your life in his or her hands. Know your spotter and his or her capabilities. Determine whether your spotter is easily distracted or knows how to spot, or perhaps he or she is too weak to safely handle the weight. If you have the slightest doubt concerning your spotter, get another one, or an additional one. If someone volunteers to spot you but you don't know the person or have little faith in his or her abilities, politely refuse the offer and get someone you trust. If you are worried about your safety, you cannot get a good workout. Be a good spotter yourself. Earn the reputation of being safety conscious and you will become the person that others seek out as a training partner and spotter.

Selecting a Training Partner

The ideal training partner would be someone who is trustworthy, punctual, knowledgeable, sincere, similar to you in lifting abilities, close in age, and the same gender. However, the perfect partner is not always waiting for you to appear in the weight room, so look for the best partner you can get. I have had many good training partners who did not fit these criteria, and I was happy to have them. I learned something from every one of them, and I hope they learned from me.

The person you select should also choose you as a training partner so that both of you will feel comfortable with the relationship. You will spend as much as six to eight hours per week together so you must be compatible. Having the same interests, such as type of job, could be a good thing or a bad thing. The good thing about this is that you have something interesting to talk about during the brief rest periods, but the bad thing is that you might talk too much and neglect your workout. You need to remember to maintain your concentration during your workout.

Your workout partner should be able to give and take constructive criticism without being too harsh. If you feel that your partner's criticism is meant as an insult, discuss this with your partner and let him know your feelings. He probably did not realize how he was coming across to you and will change immediately.

Using Assistive Equipment

Assistive equipment is anything that helps the lifter that is not part of his or her own body, such as a body suit, a bench press shirt, knee wraps, lifting briefs, a lifting belt, footwear, wrist wraps, gymnastics chalk, baby powder, and smelling salts. This subject will be discussed in detail in chapter 7, Lifting Ergogenics.

General Rules of Powerlifting

The International Powerlifting Federation (IPF) has a set of general rules that other powerlifting organizations agree with. The other organizations are the Natural Athlete's Strength Association (NASA), USA Powerlifting (USAPL), and the Amateur Athletic Union (AAU). These rules will be listed here but you should consult the rulebook of the organization you are competing in for specific rules. Throughout these rules, wherever "he" or "his" occur, such reference applies to either sex.

1. A. The International Powerlifting Federation recognizes the following lifts, which must be taken in the same sequence in all competitions conducted under the IPF rules:

   1. Squat

   2. Bench press

   3. Deadlift

   4. Total

   B. Competition takes place between lifters in categories defined by sex, body weight, and age. The Men's and Women's Open Championships permit lifters of any age in excess of 14 years.

   C. The rules apply to all levels of competition whether it be World, Regional, International, or any competition that states that it is conducted under IPF rules.

   D. Each competitor is allowed three attempts on each lift. Any exceptions are explained in the appropriate section of the rulebook. The lifter's best valid attempt on each lift, disregarding any fourth attempts for record purposes, counts toward his competition total. The winner of a category shall be the lifter who achieves the highest total. The remaining lifters shall be ranked in descending order of total. Lifters failing to achieve a total are eliminated from the competition. If two or more lifters achieve the same total weight, the lighter lifter ranks above the heavier lifter.

2. The IPF through its member federations conducts and sanctions the following World Championships:

   Men's Open World Championships

   Women's Open World Championships

   Men's and Women's Combined Junior World Championships

   Men's and Women's Combined Master World Championships

   Bench Press World Championships

3. The IPF also recognizes and registers world records for the same lifts within the categories described hereunder:

Age categories

Men

1. Senior: From 14 years upward (some of the U.S.-based federations and associations have lowered the minimum age qualifications for participation in sanctioned competitions)

2. Junior: From 14 years to and including 23 years of age

3. Master I: From 40 years to and including 49 years of age

4. Master II: From 50 years upward

Women

1. Junior: From 14 years to and including 23 years of age

2. Senior: From 14 years upward

3. Master: From 40 years upward

Competitive lifting shall be restricted to competitors aged 14 years and over. The lifter must have attained minimum age on the day of the competition where age limits are imposed. A lifter may remain in the junior category throughout the full calendar year in which he reaches the stated upper limit of that category.

Age grouping for Master lifters is determined by their actual birth date.

Men over 60 years of age competing in the "from 50 years upward" and women over 50 years of age competing in the "from 40 years upward" categories shall be eligible for first-, second-, and third-place medals based on their Schwartz/Malone formula. (This formula is considered obsolete by the IPF and has been replaced by the Wilks formula. However, not all federations and associations have made the change, despite the fact that Dr. Schwartz has indicated that his formula is overdue for correction.) This will not affect the competition point scoring system of their placing within the "from 50 years upward" category for men and the "from 40 years upward" category for women.

Age categories and their further subdivisions may be adapted for use nationally at the discretion of the national federation.

Body Weight Categories

Men

1. Less than 52 kg up to 52 kg

2. 56-kg class: 52.01 to 56 kg

3. 60-kg class: 56.01 to 60 kg

4. 67.5-kg class: 60.01 to 67.5 kg

5. 75-kg class: 67.51 to 75 kg

6. 82.5-kg class: 75.01 to 82.5 kg

7. 90-kg class: 82.51 to 90 kg

8. 100-kg class: 90.01 to 100 kg

9. 110-kg class: 100.01 to 110 kg

10. 125-kg class: 110.01 to 125 kg

11. 125+ kg class: 125.01 to unlimited

Women

1. Less than 44 kg up to 44 kg

2. 48-kg class: 44.01 to 48 kg

3. 52-kg class: 48.01 to 52 kg

4. 56-kg class: 52.01 to 56 kg

5. 60-kg class: 56.01 to 60 kg

6. 67.5-kg class: 60.01 to 67.5 kg

7. 75-kg class: 67.51 to 75 kg

8. 82.5-kg class: 75.01 to 82.5 kg

9. 90-kg class: 82.51 to 90 kg

10. 90+ kg class: 90.01 to unlimited

Note: Lifters with disabilities have different starting and ending body weight limits than other lifters.

4. Each nation is allowed a maximum of 11 competitors distributed throughout the range of the 11 body weight categories for men and ten competitors throughout the range of 10 body weight categories for women. There must not be more than two competitors from one nation in any particular body weight category.

However, women's master lifters may be entered to a maximum of nine competitors distributed throughout the three combined body weight categories of 44-52 kg, 56-67.5 kg, and 75-90+ kg. Not more than three competitors from any nation shall be in any particular combined body weight categories.

5. Each nation is allowed a maximum of two alternates or reserves. These alternates or reserves may be substituted at any time prior to the commencement of the weigh-in for a body weight category. Each nation must submit a team roster giving the name of each lifter, a body weight category, and highest total achieved at

national or international level during the previous 12 months. The date and title of the competition in which the best total was achieved must also be stated.

The details must be submitted to the responsible official prior to the commencement of the weigh-in for the lowest weight category, i.e., 52 kg for men and 44 kg for women. The names of the alternates or reserves with their body weight categories and best totals must also be submitted at this time.

6.   Point scoring for all World, Continental, and Regional Championships shall be 12, 9, 8, 7, 5, 4, 3, and 2 for the first eight placing in any body weight category. Thereafter, each lifter who makes a total in the competition shall be awarded 1 point. Point scoring for all national competitions shall be at the discretion of the national federation.

7.   Only the point scores of the six best lifters of each nation will be counted for the team competition at all international championships. In the case of a tie in points scored, a final team placing shall be decided as described for team awards in item 10.

8.   Any nation having been a member of the IPF for more than three years should endeavor to include at least one international referee among its team officials at world championships. If a referee from that nation is not present or, if present, does not officiate during the championships, then only the four best lifters from that nation will be counted for the team competition.

9.   Teams shall be nominated to the Secretary of the IPF or Region and also the Meet Director at least 21 days before the commencement date of the championships. Failure to comply with this requirement may result in disqualification of the offending team.

10.   Team awards shall be given to the first three places. In the case of a tie in the classification of a team or a nation, the team having the largest number of first places will be ranked first. In the case of a tie between two nations having the same number of first places, the one having the most second places will be classified first, and so on through the placings of the six scoring lifters.

Summary

This chapter gives you an overall look at the sport of powerlifting, including rules and regulations, tips on choosing a workout facility and finding a training partner, and the physiology of muscle gains. Reread this chapter after you have ventured into the world of powerlifting and you will discover something useful each time.

2

Squat

It is generally agreed among elite powerlifters that the squat is the ultimate conditioner or test of strength. O'Shea and Wegner (*Physician and Sports Medicine*, 96: 109-120, 1981) stated that "the full squat must be considered the cornerstone exercise, because it quickly stimulates overall strength increases in both men and women. Neglecting this exercise retards overall development and prevents the athlete from achieving optimal performance." This is true of athletes in all sports, not just powerlifters.

You have probably heard that squats are bad for your knees. However, only one researcher, K.K. Klein (*Journal of the Association for Physical and Mental Rehabilitation*, 15(1): 6-11, 1961) has ever reported that full squats with weights were bad for your knees. Mr. Klein was probably talking about the deep knee bend where the lifter's weight is on the balls of his feet and knees are in front of his feet. Subsequent research has shown that the squat does not affect medial (inside) and lateral (outside) knee stability, rotational stability, or anterior (front) and posterior (back) knee stability. Although Klein's work has often been challenged, people still use his opinion as an excuse not to do squats. A survey of national and international weightlifters and powerlifters conducted by Herrick et al. (*Powerlifting USA*, 7(5): 7-9, 1983) found that although lifters reported more knee pain, they experienced less clinical or symptomatic arthritis.

People who lift three times their own body weight are common in powerlifting, and those who win national and world titles lift more than that. This is particularly true with the smaller lifters, including the 198-pound class. There have been reports of people lifting 800 to 1,000 pounds. Larger lifters routinely break the 1,000-pound barrier in many national and world-class meets. If you are new to powerlifting and strength training, you probably think that there is no way that someone like you could ever squat while bearing a lot of weight. Not true. No matter what your age is, you can train yourself to be stronger than you ever thought possible if you are willing to pay the price. The price in this instance means to follow a regimen of proper training, proper diet, adequate amounts of rest, and perfecting the proper techniques. You should also realize that the great squatters of today did not achieve their success overnight, but through months and years of constant and consistent training even when they had something else to do, did not feel like going to the gym, or thought of any other excuse.

Even if you have no plans of competing in powerlifting, there are many benefits of practicing the squat. Here are some major benefits to participating in a squat program:

- It stimulates optimal physical growth and development in the young athlete.

- It increases bone density along with a corresponding increase in ligament and tendon strength that produces greater joint stability.

- It develops the large muscle groups—the lower back, hips, buttocks, and thighs—usually called the body's "power zone."

- It increases neuromuscular efficiency, making for an excellent transfer of power to other similar movements requiring jumping for height, broad jumping, quick starts, fast stops, all forms of running, throwing, lifting, and pushing with the lower body.

Mechanics of the Squat

To describe the proper mechanical techniques of the squat, it must be broken into three segments—preparation, descent, and ascent.

PREPARATION

Position the bar on the squat racks to approximately mid-chest height. Grasp the bar with an overhand grip wider than your shoulders with either a closed (thumbs around the bar) or open (thumbs not around the bar) grip (see figures 2.1 and 2.2). After securing the proper grip, duck under the bar between your hands; this will place you directly in the middle with the weight balanced on your back. The bar should be positioned on the mass of your back no more than 1½ inches (3 centimeters) below the top of the shoulders with the hands positioned as close to the shoulders as your chest and shoulder flexibility will allow (see figure 2.3). The hands should be used to press the bar against the back and *not* to support the weight. Your elbows should be pulled back and lifted up,

Figure 2.1   In the closed overhand grip the thumbs go around the bar.

Figure 2.2   In the open overhand grip the thumbs stay with the fingers and do not go around the bar.

Figure 2.3   In the correct bar position, place the hands as close to the shoulders as possible.

pushing forward with the hands pressing the bar into the back. In this position the arms create a rack to help support the bar. Your head should be up, facing straight ahead throughout the exercise. Your chest should be up and out, shoulders pulled back, with shoulder blades pulled close together. The spinal muscles, from neck to hips, should be in a strong isometric contraction, making the back flat with a rigid swayback at the base near the hips (see figure 2.4). The feet should be flat on the floor and spaced wider than the shoulders, with the toes turned out 15 to 30 degrees (see figure 2.5).

Figure 2.4 The back should be flat with a rigid swayback at the base near the hips.

Figure 2.5 Place the feet flat on the floor, farther apart than shoulder-width, and turn the toes out slightly.

Immediately before the descent, isometrically contract all the muscles in the upper thighs and torso. This activates the stretch reflex mechanisms, which assist in producing a strong eccentric contraction of the muscles involved in the descent. A muscle produces a much stronger contraction whenever it is stretched just before contraction.

DESCENT

After taking a deep breath and pressing your abdominal muscles firmly against your belt, start the descent by sticking your buttocks out and begin to descend as if to sit on a bench. Continue to squat down, in a slow and controlled manner, to a position slightly lower than parallel (see figure 2.6). This is when the bend in the leg at the thigh is lower than the top of the leg at the knee. Throughout this exercise the weight should stay over the middle of the feet or the heels, and not over the toes. The knees should only move slightly forward and never farther than the toes.

Figure 2.6 During the descent phase, squat to a position slightly lower than parallel.

During the descent, avoid excessive forward lean of the torso by keeping the hips under the bar as much as possible. The forward lean is considered excessive if it is 30 degrees or more. If the bar is placed low on the back, there is a tendency for the trunk to lean forward to keep the bar from rolling down the back (see figure 2.7). This can be minimized by keeping the hips under the bar as long as possible. Keeping the hips under the bar also puts the quadriceps in a position to initiate the ballistic drive out of the bottom position. You can generate a lot more force with your legs than you can with your back and it is also much safer.

Figure 2.7 The author demonstrates excessive forward lean of the torso, which can result from the bar being placed too low on the back.

ASCENT

Begin the transition from the descent to the ascent with a powerful drive to accelerate out of the bottom position using strong quadriceps extension. At the same time, thrust the head back to benefit from a strong contraction of the trapezius muscles. Press firmly against the belt with the abdominal muscles. This action will keep the upper body from leaning forward, and it will keep the weight over the hips to initiate upward movement. Once upward movements have started, begin to strongly contract and push the hips forward under the bar. After passing through the most difficult part (about 30 degrees above parallel), begin to breathe out through the mouth, avoiding the Valsalva effect (holding the breath while straining), which could cause you to pass out. Make sure you complete the lift with the torso in an upright position with the knees locked. You can attain this position by flexing and pushing forward with your hips while pressing your heels against the floor.

Support Work for the Squat

The following exercises should be done to work the muscles used in the squat. For exercise instructions, see pages 116 through 129.

1. Calf (sitting)
2. Calf (standing)
3. Quadriceps extension
4. Hamstring flexion
5. Sled
6. Lunge with no weights
7. Lunge with weights

Should the Squat Be Eliminated From Competition?

After reading how to do the squat and attempting to follow the directions, you have already discovered that it is a complicated exercise with an element of danger to it. Based on this, there are those in powerlifting who are trying to have the squat eliminated from competition. Before we eliminate the squat I think we should first consider the value the squat has for other sports requiring strength, such as football and track and field, and for sports requiring lower body joint stability to prevent injury, such as soccer and ice hockey. Many who first begin to train for these reasons suddenly realize that they are good enough to enter competition, and in many cases continue to compete for many years. Before eliminating this valuable exercise from competition, we should weigh the pros and cons. In my opinion, the con side's argument is injury, which could be eliminated by learning and practicing proper technique and safety procedures. I believe that the value received from doing this exercise far outweighs the reasons for eliminating it and thus, the squat should remain an important part of powerlifting.

Most Common Mistakes

In a round-table discussion reported in the May/June 1993 issue of the *NSCA Journal*, the eight most common errors of the squat were discussed. The participants are well known, successful, and highly regarded as lifters and strength coaches: Doug Fairchild, USWF senior coach; Bert Hill, Detroit Lions Inc. strength and conditioning coach; Meg Ritchie, University of Arizona strength and conditioning coach; and Dave Sochor, Doniphan High School NE strength coach. Although they generally agreed on the eight most common errors, they did not agree on the order of importance. From this I think we can conclude that there is no one most important error but that all errors must be eliminated or minimized in order to be an outstanding lifter. The eight errors are discussed as follows:

1. Failure to reach parallel with the anterior surface of the thigh. This results in inferior overall leg development. This will also result in a bad habit that will cause "red lights" (failure) in a meet.

2. Excessive forward lean (more than 30 degrees) as the lifter begins to descend (see figure 2.7, page 20). This is usually the result of lack of overall strength, especially a weak lower back.

Squat **23**

3. Knees traveling forward (figure 2.8). This places undue pressure on the knee joint.

4. Heels coming off the floor at the lower part of the lift. This creates a loss of balance, unstable positioning, and unreasonable pressure on the knee.

Figure 2.8 The knees are too far forward, placing extra pressure on the knee joints.

5. Improper bar placement (figures 2.9 and 2.10). If the bar is too high, it will cause undue stress on the lower back. If the bar is too low, it will cause the lifter to bend over to keep the bar from rolling down the back.

Figure 2.9 Bar placement too high.

Figure 2.10 Bar placement too low.

6. Incorrect head position (figures 2.11 and 2.12). If the head position is too high, it could cause loss of balance. If it is too low, it will cause a rounding of the back, in turn causing the bar to roll forward during the lowest point of the lift.

Figure 2.11 Head position too high.

Figure 2.12 Head position too low.

7. Incorrect foot placement (figures 2.13 and 2.14). If the feet are too close together, the stress will be on the quadriceps and lower back, making it difficult for the hamstrings and gluteal (buttocks) muscles to aid in the lift. If the feet are too far apart, the lifter will lose some of the upward thrust trying to get the legs back under to complete the lift.

Figure 2.13 Feet are too close together.

8. Improper breathing. The lungs should be filled with air during the descent and most of the ascent to give support to the back.

Figure 2.14 Feet are too far apart.

Helpful Suggestions

1. Do your warm-up squats the same way you do in training. Don't leave your best lift in the warm-up room; save it for the contest.

2. Be completely focused on your squat, have a mental image of exactly how you will do it, and *never* allow a negative thought to enter your mind.

The positioning of the feet and bar is usually a topic of discussion and debate among powerlifters. The suggestions offered here are the usual placements suggested for beginning powerlifters and are also used by national and world-class lifters. However, we all have our own unique physique. Here are the various combinations of leg and torso length that I have observed:

- Short legs with short torso
- Short legs with long torso
- Long legs with short torso
- Long legs with long torso
- Medium-length legs with medium-length torso

Some lifters and coaches recommend a different foot and bar placement for each combination. A person with a short torso should use the high bar position or at least start in this position and adjust from there. A person with a long torso should use a low bar position placed on the trapezius (upper back) and posterior deltoid muscles (back of shoulders) as a starting position.

The length of the legs should have no effect on the bar placement but should dictate the foot placement. Longer legs should be placed as wide as possible to allow the greatest possible upward thrust. This could be shoulder-width or much wider depending on what proves to be best. Remember, the narrower the stance, the higher you are, and the greater the distance you have to squat.

For those who have proportionate leg and torso length, you should experiment with both the high bar and low bar position and then make adjustments that suit your needs. The position should be determined by how far you need to lean forward. The bar must stay over the feet or you will fall or struggle to keep your balance by putting excessive stress on the lower back and knees.

Competitive Rules of Performance for the Squat
(NASA Rulebook and USAPL)

1. The lifter shall assume an upright position with the top of the bar not more than 1½ inches (3 centimeters) below the top of the anterior deltoids. The bar shall be held horizontally across the shoulders with the hands and fingers gripping the bar and the feet flat on the platform with the knees locked.

2. After removing the bar from the racks, the lifter must move backward to establish his or her position. The lifter shall wait in this position for the chief referee's signal. The signal shall be given as soon as the lifter is motionless and erect with the knees locked and the bar properly positioned. If mechanical racks that withdraw are used, the lifter must remove the barbell from the racks before they are withdrawn and wait motionless for the chief referee's signal. The chief referee's signal shall consist of a downward movement of the arm and the audible command "squat."

3. Upon receiving the chief referee's signal, the lifter must bend the knees and lower the body until the top surface of the legs at the hip joint is lower than the top of the knees.

4. The lifter must recover at will without double bouncing or any downward movement to an upright position with the knees locked. When the lifter is motionless, the chief referee will give the signal to replace the bar.

5. The signal to replace the bar will consist of a backward motion of the hand and the audible command "rack."

6. The lifter shall face the front of the platform.

7. The lifter shall not hold the collars, sleeves, or discus at any time during the performance of the lift. However, the edge of the hands gripping the bar may be in contact with the inner surface of the collars.

8. Not more than five and not less than two spotter/loaders shall be on the platform at any time.

9. The lifter may enlist the help of the spotter/loaders in removing the bar from the racks. However, once the bar has cleared the racks, the spotter/loaders shall not assist the lifter further with regard to proper positioning, foot placement, bar positioning, and so on.

10. The lifter may, at the chief referee's discretion, be given an additional attempt at the same weight if failure in an attempt was due to an error by one or more of the spotter/loaders.

Causes for Disqualification of a Squat

1. Failure to observe the chief referee's signals at the commencement or completion of a lift.

2. Double bouncing or more than one recovery attempt at the bottom of the lift.

3. Failure to assume an upright position with the knees locked at the commencement and completion of the lift.

4. Any shuffling of the feet laterally, backward, or forward, during the performance of the lift.

5. Failure to bend the knees and lower the body until the top surface of the legs at the hip joint is lower than the top of the knees.

6. Changing the position of the bar across the shoulders after the commencement of the lift.

7. Contact with the bar by the spotter/loaders between the referee's signals.

8. Contact of elbows or upper arms with the legs.

9. Failure to make a bona fide attempt to return the bar to the racks.

10. Any intentional dropping or dumping of the bar.

Summary

The squat is considered the best overall strengthener and conditioner of the three lifts. The position and the muscles developed are used in many sports, such as football and track and field. The squat is one of the hardest lifts to master and can be dangerous if the proper techniques and safety precautions are not strictly followed. Start light and increase weight slowly with this lift, with a long-term goal of steady progression to impressive weights. It will happen if you don't give up!

Bench Press

3

The most admired lifters in both bodybuilding and powerlifting are the big benchers. "How much can you bench?" is the first question people will ask when you tell them you are a weightlifter. This exercise is popular because of the muscles it develops, and the bench press technique is easy to learn compared to the other lifts in powerlifting competition. The bench press develops the chest muscles (pectorals), the back of the upper arm (triceps), and the front of the shoulder (anterior deltoid). When properly developed, these muscles contribute a great deal to an attractive upper body for both men and women.

Mechanics of the Bench Press

Like the squat, the mechanics of the bench press will also be broken into three segments—preparation, descent, and ascent.

PREPARATION

Begin by sitting down on the far end of the bench with your back to the upright supports. Now lie back and position yourself so that your buttocks, shoulders, and head are firmly and squarely on the bench. Your legs should straddle the bench, and your feet should be flat on the floor, about shoulder-width apart or wider (figure 3.1). This position will provide you with the stability necessary to perform a good bench press. Your eyes should be in line with the front edge of the shelf where the bar is racked, not directly under the bar (figure 3.2). Grip the bar in an overhand closed grip (thumbs around bar), with the hands in the same position on both sides, and about shoulder-width apart or wider. Do not use the open hand grip, because it is dangerous and can lead to wrist problems after a few years of lifting (see figure 3.3). An appropriate grip width on the bar will position the wrist directly above the elbows as the bar touches the chest. With help from your spotter, take the bar from the rack and push to a straight elbow position. You should be supported mostly by your upper back and feet. Your lower back should be arched with your buttocks fully contracted and very lightly touching the bench.

Figure 3.1 Straddle the bench, with the feet flat on the floor.

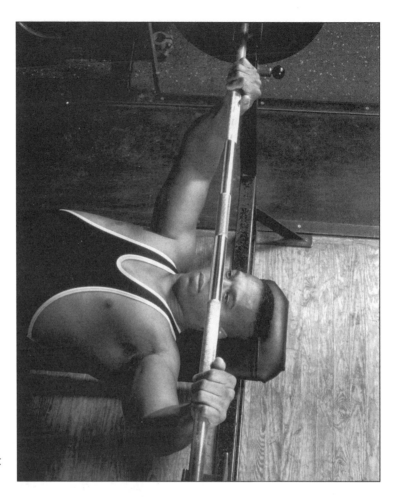

Figure 3.2 Align your eyes with the front edge of the shelf where the bar is racked.

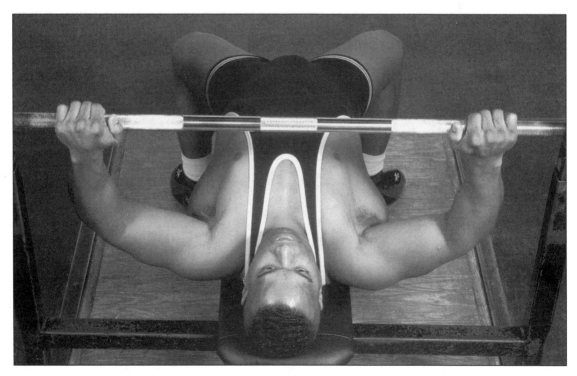

Figure 3.3 The open hand grip shown here is not recommended because it can lead to wrist problems.

DESCENT

Pause with the bar in an extended arm position. Inhale, expanding the chest as much as possible and hold, and then slowly lower the bar to your chest. The bar should make contact with the highest point of the chest, usually located approximately 1 inch above or below the nipples (figure 3.4). While lowering the bar, try to push the chest upward to meet the bar. This will cause the shoulder blades to pull closer together and the pectorals to stretch (load up), which causes a stronger contraction as you start your upward movement. The elbows should not be close to the ribs, which would force the triceps to do most of the work, or straight out from the shoulders, which would force the pectorals to do most of the work. The elbows

Figure 3.4 During the descent phase, lower the bar to the highest point of the chest.

should be at a 45-degree angle between the rib cage and the shoulders to get the maximum effort from both muscle groups (figure 3.5).

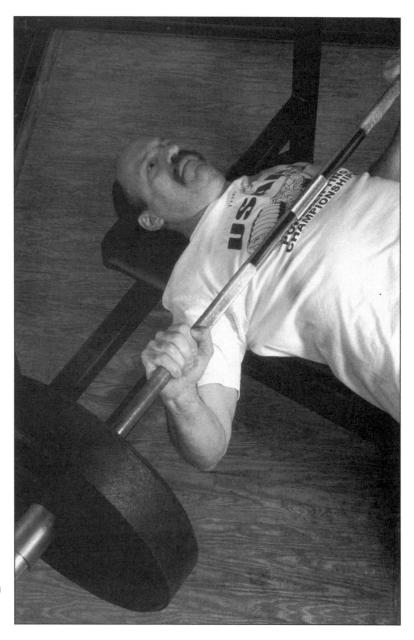

Figure 3.5 The elbows should be at a 45-degree angle between the rib cage and the shoulders.

ASCENT

Once the bar touches your chest, explode upward, creating momentum to go through the sticking point (most difficult part), which is usually about halfway up. You should exhale immediately after passing through this point. Continue pushing straight upward until your elbows are locked out.

Hand Width

The biggest difference among lifters doing the bench press is the width of hand placement on the bar. Many will take the widest grip allowed, where they place the forefinger on the ring, which must be covered. This shortens the distance for the bar to travel and favors people with strong pectoral muscles and anterior deltoids. Some will take a narrow grip, in which the little finger is about two finger widths inside the rings. This grip increases the distance the bar must travel and puts a great stress on the triceps muscles. Only people with exceptionally strong triceps should use this technique. Beginners should start with hands shoulder width apart and then begin to experiment with various widths until they find the one that best suits them.

Support Work for the Bench Press

The following exercises will develop the muscles used in the bench press. For exercise instructions, see pages 116 through 129.

1. Wide grip bench press

2. Narrow grip bench press

3. Nose breakers

4. Dumbbell flies

5. Dumbbell press

6. Front dumbbell raise

7. Press down on lat bar (triceps)

Most Common Mistakes

1. Lowering the bar too slowly to the chest. If you take too long to lower the bar to your chest, you are wasting energy and strength needed to raise the bar back to a straight arm position.

2. Lowering the bar too quickly to the chest. If you allow the bar to drop too quickly, you will waste energy and strength controlling the bar as it nears your chest.

3. Exhaling during the descent. You should inhale fully, expanding the chest as much as possible.

4. Moving or shuffling the feet during exercise. Positioning your feet while sitting on the bench and placing most of your weight on your feet and shoulders will control movement.

Helpful Suggestions

The ready position

1. Chalk. Apply chalk to the hands to maintain a good grip and to the upper back to prevent slipping on the bench.

2. Feet. Position the feet while sitting on the edge of the bench and keep them flat and planted throughout the lift.

3. Shoulders. Shoulders should be evenly spaced on the bench.

4. Weight. Most of the weight should be on the shoulders and feet.

5. Buttocks. Your buttocks should only lightly touch the bench.

Descent

1. Breathing. Take a large breath of air before lowering the bar, keeping the chest expanded.

2. Bar speed. Lower the bar slowly to the proper spot on the chest, slightly above the nipples.

3. Bar movement. Stop the bar as quickly as possible to avoid delay of the press command.

Ascent

1. The blastoff. Drive off the chest with maximum effort to create momentum in order to pass through the sticking point.

2. Bar movement. Exert maximum effort throughout the lift to a lockout position.

3. Lockout. Maintain a lockout position until the referee gives the "rack" command.

Key points

1. Use a wide grip. This shortens the distance the bar has to travel.

2. Maximize the arch of your back. This shortens the distance the bar has to travel.

3. Use maximum breath. This expands the chest and shortens the distance the bar has to travel.

4. Slow, controlled descent. Keep control of the bar while hitting proper position on the chest (sweet spot).

Competitive Rules of Performance for the Bench Press (USAPL, formerly ADFPA Rulebook)

1. The lifter must lie on the back with head, shoulders, and buttocks in contact with the flat bench surface. Feet must be flat on the floor. This position must be maintained throughout the attempt once the "press" signal has been given.

2. To achieve firm footing, the lifter may use plates or blocks not exceeding 7 inches (18 centimeters) in height and 17.7 inches (45 × 45 centimeters) in length and width. The entire foot must be flat on the surface.

3. The lifter may have a liftoff from the spotter or coach, which must be taken at arms' length, not at the chest.

4. The spacing of the hands may not exceed 31⅞ inches (81 centimeters) measured between the forefingers. A reverse grip is permitted, provided that the distance between the little fingers does not exceed 81 centimeters.

5. After receiving the bar at arms' length, the lifter will remain motionless until the signal is given. The signal will consist of the audible command "press." Before receiving the signal, the lifter may make any position adjustments without penalty.

6. After receiving the signal, the lifter lowers the bar until it touches the chest. It must completely stop before it can be pressed back to a straight arm position and held motionless until the audible command "rack" is given.

7. The bar is allowed to stop during the upward motion but is NOT allowed any downward movement of either or both hands.

Causes for Disqualification of a Bench Press

1. Failure to observe the signals at the commencement or completion of the lift.

2. Any change in the elected lifting position during the lift (i.e., any raising of the head, shoulders, buttocks, or feet from their points of contact with the bench or platform/blocks, or lateral movement of the body or the hand on the bar once the "press" signal has been given).

3. Heaving or bouncing the bar off the chest.

4. Any uneven extension of the arms at the completion of the lift.

5. Any downward movement of either hand as the bar is being pressed upward.

6. The bar may stop; if in the opinion of the referee, the safety of the lifter is in jeopardy, the "rack" signal will be given.

7. Contact with the bar by spotter/loaders between the chief referee's signals.

8. Contact of the lifter's feet with the bench or its supports.

9. Deliberate contact between the bar and the bar rest uprights during the lift, which would aid the press.

Summary

The bench press is a favorite lift for beginners because the results are noticeable in a short amount of time. It is also the easiest lift to learn and master the proper techniques. If you have a good spotter, the possibility of injury is low. The muscles developed through the bench press are not only visually attractive but they give protection to the vital chest area and help to stabilize the shoulder and elbow joints.

4

Deadlift

The deadlift is one of the best tests of overall body strength, and has been used for training strength athletes for years. The deadlift is the last of the three lifts in powerlifting competition, making it the one that, in many cases, determines who wins or loses.

The deadlift has two styles that are used at all levels of competition. The styles are called the *regular stance deadlift* and the *sumo stance deadlift*. (There is no information available, to my knowledge, that indicates which form is used more often and which one is more successful.) When performing the regular stance, the lifter's feet are close together, less than shoulder-width apart, and the hands are placed outside the legs. The sumo stance is performed with the feet wider than the shoulders, like a sumo wrestler's stance, and the hands are placed inside the legs.

Regular Stance

This form starts with the lifter approaching the bar until the shins are touching. The feet should be a little less than shoulder-width apart, so that when the lifter squats to grasp the bar the hands should be shoulder-width apart with the arms hanging straight down from the shoulders. The forearms should lightly touch the outside of each leg to guide the hands to the proper bar position. The hands should grip the bar in an alternate grip, one palm facing forward and one facing backward, to keep the bar from rolling out of the hands (see figure 4.1). After taking the grip, the lifter should lift the head up and look straight ahead. Arms should be straight with the shoulders as high as possible. The chest should be up and out with the shoulders pulled back and the shoulder blades pulled close together (see figure 4.2a and b). This will put the lifter in a position for the legs to do the major part of the lift without undue stress on the lower back. From this position, the lifter pulls the head and shoulders back hard as he pushes against the floor with the middle to back half of the feet. The lifter then pulls the bar from the floor by first extending the knees to start the movement. As the bar passes the knees, the hips should be pushed forward as the lower back begins to extend. In the ideal lift, the knees, hips, and lower back would lock out at exactly the same time. The finishing point is attained when the knees and hips are extended and locked out and the upper and lower back are extended so that the front points of the shoulders are behind the front points of the hips (figure 4.3). The bar should touch or lightly brush the legs throughout the entire lift.

Figure 4.1 Correct hand and foot placement in the regular stance.

a

b

Figure 4.2 Regular stance start position (*a*) from the front and (*b*) from the side.

a   b

Figure 4.3 Regular stance finish position (a) from the front and (b) from the side.

Sumo Stance

The sumo deadlift starts by approaching the bar until the shins touch, with feet wider than the shoulders and turned outward between 30 and 40 degrees (figure 4.4). Width of the stance varies greatly with this form, anywhere from a slightly wider than shoulder-width stance, to a stance where the outside edges of the feet are almost touching the plates on both sides. The arms should hang straight down from the shoulders with the hands gripping the bar between the legs. In this position, the lifter's hips are lower and the back is straighter during liftoff than the regular stance (figure 4.5). The final position for the sumo lift is the same as for the standard

Figure 4.4   Correct hand and foot placement in the sumo stance.

lift. The hands will be touching the legs in front, which sometimes makes it harder to pull the shoulders back to the correct position (figure 4.6).

Lifters who are strong squatters (lifters with long trunks and short, thick legs with feet naturally turned outward) usually find that the sumo stance is the best stance to use. However, each lifter will have to experiment with the width of the feet until they find the position that works best.

How to Choose

Determining which style of stance—regular or sumo—is best suited to you is a common and difficult question for many beginning lifters. Study and experiment with the techniques for each style. Try a complete cycle with each style for about 10 to 16 weeks to determine which one will allow you to develop the most lifting power. Keep

Figure 4.5 Sumo stance start position.

Figure 4.6 Sumo stance finish position.

complete notes of each workout and plot your improvement with each style, until you are absolutely sure which one is best for you. Stick with your decision and begin to fine tune the techniques, finding all the leverages and ways to include additional muscles to aid with the lift, and amazing results will happen.

Mechanics of the Deadlift

There are five phases to the deadlift: preparation, liftoff, pull through the knees, lockout, and lowering to the floor.

PREPARATION

Approach the bar until the shins touch. Place the feet at a distance less than shoulder-width for the regular stance and wider than the shoulders for the sumo stance. The toes should be turned outward, 20 to 40 degrees, to allow for the hips to push through. Squat down with the arms hanging straight down from the shoulders, which would put them outside the legs for the regular stance and inside for the sumo stance, and take the bar in an alternate grip. The grip should be deep in the hands, with the fingers wrapped tightly around the bar. Be sure not to allow the bar to hang on the fingers, which could result in dropping the weights. After gripping the bar, lift the head up, straighten the arms, pull shoulder blades together, and lock the back in this position.

LIFTOFF

Initiate liftoff by pushing the feet into the floor, causing knee extension, which is quickly followed by hip extension (see figure 4.7). When you begin the pull from the floor, use strength or a steady pull, not an explosive jerk. If you try to jerk the bar from the floor, you will break form if the bar does not move immediately. This will cause your hips to raise due to knee extension without hip extension. This, along with rounding of the shoulders, will result in a straight leg deadlift, putting the lower back in a very dangerous position.

PULL THROUGH THE KNEES

As you move the bar up close to the knees, knee extension slows down and, at this point, hip extension (pushing the hips through) causes the main movement. Lower back extension is also necessary at this point in order to limit dangerous stress, because of the great hip extending force applied by the hamstrings and gluteals. The bar should always lightly touch the shins, kneecaps, and thighs. Do not drag the bar along the legs, especially the thighs, which could hinder the upward movement of the bar.

Figure 4.7 Liftoff position.

LOCKOUT

You accomplish the lockout through knee extension, hip extension, and upper and lower back extension; these are all coordinated to finish simultaneously. It is important to coordinate these joint actions so as to guide the bar through the most efficient path. Avoid locking the knees straight before extending the hips and back. If the knees are locked, with little hip or back extension, the bar is left dangling 2 to 8 inches from the thighs, causing increased and dangerous stress on the lower back.

LOWERING TO THE FLOOR

Begin to flex at the hips and knees, keeping the back straight and shoulders pulled back. Use the legs to complete downward movement after the bar passes the knees. Keep the bar close to the thighs, knees, and shins throughout the movement.

Support Work for the Deadlift

The following exercises should be done to work the muscles used in the deadlift. For exercise instructions, see pages 116 through 129. In addition to the exercises listed here, see also the list of support work exercises for the squat on page 21. Since the same muscles are used for the deadlift and the squat, the same exercises benefit both lifts.

1. Lunge
2. Good mornings

Most Common Mistakes

1. Not getting close enough to the bar when preparing for the lift
2. Not taking a deep breath before bending to grip the bar
3. Letting air out in the down position
4. Letting the head drop forward instead of pulling backward
5. Knee extension ahead of the hips and lower back
6. Letting the shoulders drop forward
7. Trying to jerk the bar from the floor
8. Not pulling the shoulders back at the completion of the lift

Helpful Suggestions

1. Approach the bar until your shins touch.
2. Make sure your feet are evenly spaced on each side.
3. Keep your shoulders up and back with shoulder blades pulled together.
4. Keep your head up, looking straight ahead.
5. Keep your shoulders high and your hips low.
6. Make sure your hands are evenly spaced on the bar.
7. Keep the bar against your legs as you stand up.
8. Flex and thrust your hips through as soon as the bar clears your knees.
9. To be certain you are legally locked out, press your heels against the floor and tighten and push your gluteals forward while pulling your shoulders back.

Competitive Rules for the Deadlift
(USAPL, formerly ADFPA Rulebook)

1. The bar must be lifted upward until the lifter is standing with knees locked. Stopping of the bar is allowed, but no downward movement is permitted following a stop.

2. On completion of the lift, the knees are locked and shoulders held in an erect position (not forward or rounded).

3. The chief referee's signal shall consist of a downward movement of the hand and the audible command "down." The signal will not be given until the bar is held motionless and the lifter is in the apparent finished position.

4. Any raising of the bar from the platform or any deliberate attempt to do so will count as an attempt.

Causes for Disqualification of a Deadlift

1. Any downward movement of the bar during the uplifting.

2. Failure to stand erect with shoulders held in an erect position.

3. Failure to lock the knees at the completion of the lift.

4. Any secondary knee flexion; once the bar has started upward, the knees must continuously extend without additional bending at the knees.

5. Supporting the bar on the thighs during the performance of the lift; the bar must continue to move upward on the thighs, not rest on the thighs as the knees straighten.

6. Any lateral movement of the feet or stepping forward or backward.

7. Lowering the bar before receiving the referee's signal.

8. Allowing the bar to return to the platform without maintaining control with both hands.

Summary

This chapter presents the deadlift techniques for both the regular stance and the sumo stance. The choice of stance is an individual issue; you should experiment with both to find out which works best for you. The deadlift is the most functional lift of the three. The techniques apply to everyday life through such actions as lifting objects from the floor. The muscles developed through the deadlift stabilize almost all the joints and the larger muscles provide padding and protection from injury during participation in contact sports. At first the techniques may appear easy, but as you progress to higher amounts of weight you will have to fine tune your movements to get the most out of every muscle.

The Training Cycle

5

There is a lot of controversy surrounding what constitutes the most effective training methods in weightlifting. Individual lifters, including world-class champions, have their own ways of training. What does this mean to a beginner or to someone who wants to train with the assurance that they are using the best method? Does it mean that there is no one perfect method of training for everyone? That is exactly what it means—each lifter has to start with the basics and develop their own training program. You can develop a program that will make you a champion if you follow a program based on the latest scientific research, carefully analyze successful programs of champions, and be willing to experiment with different methods.

Training Secrets

You might believe that powerlifting champions have a secret, magical formula; however, all the champions I know are more than willing to share their secrets with the powerlifting world. I can give you their secrets in a short list:

- Knowledge
- Dedication
- Sacrifice
- Honesty
- Confidence

Knowledge

Know the latest scientific research concerning strength development, nutrition, and the proper use of supplements. Be certain that the research you read is performed by people who have no bias for a certain outcome. For example, research conducted by a vitamin or supplement company might not give you all the data. Vitamin and supplement companies are interested in selling their products. True researchers are not biased about the outcome; they are interested in the accuracy and truthfulness of their research. Ask an informed friend or do your own research from credible, unbiased sources to educate yourself.

Dedication

You will never become strong and successful from good intentions or good excuses. A membership to a club, the right clothes and equipment, and the most elaborate program that outlines the sets, repetitions, and amount of weight will not add one ounce of muscle to your body or increase your strength. Neither will talk about your training program and reading all the powerlifting magazines contribute to your strength unless you practice the information. You must be dedicated to your program, set aside time for workouts, and don't let anything or anyone, except illness or a tragedy, keep you from it.

Sacrifice

You cannot use any type of recreational drugs, including tobacco and alcohol, and become really strong. You must have appropriate rest for your body to become stronger. This means no late-night parties with only two or three hours of sleep. Don't believe the people who claim to be able to stay up all night, drink alcohol, use recreational drugs, and still train hard and become stronger—it is not possible. If you eat the right foods in the proper combinations and quantities, get the right amount of rest, and follow a good training program, your body will thrive and become stronger.

Honesty

Be honest with yourself when you work out. I have observed people in the weight room that have used the easiest way of doing everything. They go from exercise to exercise using their "cheating" methods and then complain when they don't experience the gains that honest lifters do. Do every exercise and repetition you are supposed to do with perfect technique even if no one is watching. You know better than anyone if you cheated in your training.

Confidence

Believe in yourself. The best book I have read about this is *On Becoming World Class* (Solaris, 1996) by Dr. Judd Biasiotto with Marilyn Johnson-Littler. I recommend reading this book as part of your program, regardless of your skill level. You will gain inspiration from the book's message. Strength is a mental process: if you believe you can do the lift, you can, and if you don't believe you can do the lift, you can't. Researchers have shown that you will reach your psychological limit (mind) before you reach your physiological limit (muscle). An example of this is when extreme anger or fear overrides the psychological limit and extraordinary feats of strength are performed. You have probably heard stories of the grandmother who lifted the corner of a car off her grandson, a twin lifting a bulldozer off his brother, and my own personal experience was lifting an overturned pickup truck off my cousin when I was 12 years old. Some lifters are able to "psych up" through various processes and push past the psychological limit. This will be discussed in detail in chapter 9.

Cycling

The term *cycling* means to change the intensity of training throughout the program from light to moderate to heavy and back to light and so forth. The body should not be trained the same way all the time. Physical and mental burnout will occur as well as increased injuries. A cycle can be as long as four years when training for the Olympics or as short as a few weeks when preparing for a local contest. Olympians train for an event or events four years in the future. Although the event is four years away, they have planned their training to peak at the right time. However, within this four-year cycle there are mini-cycles and short-term goals that allow them to assess their training to see if it is working the way they had planned. These mini-cycles include a variation in weight, repetitions, number of sets, and amount of rest time between sets. For example, if you started your light cycle with a weight that you could perform for 12 repetitions, you would keep your rest time between sets no more than 90 seconds and you should do at least 5 sets in addition to warm-up sets. After a period of time, usually from two to four weeks, you would change your cycle by increasing the weight so that you can only do 8 repetitions per set, which would be the moderate phase of the cycle. You would still do 5 sets, not counting the warm-up sets, with no more than two minutes of rest between sets. After another two to four weeks, you would enter the heavy phase of the cycle. This would be a weight that you could do at least 3 but not more than 5 repetitions per set. You should only do 2 or 3 sets at the highest weight because you probably used more warm-up sets working up to the workout weight. You should take from three to five minutes of rest between sets during the heavy phase.

A cycle like the one described here should be used, in some form, throughout your lifting career. You have completed a cycle; so what happens now? Do a "max out" to determine how much you have improved, then start over again, but this time the amount of weight, at all three phases, should be increased because of the added strength you have gained during the last cycle. For example, if you were lifting 100 pounds during the light phase, you would move up to 105 or 110. If you were lifting 120 pounds for the moderate phase, you would move up to 125 or 130 pounds, and if you were doing 140 for the heavy phase, you would move up to 145 or 150 pounds.

Weight Selection

How do you determine how much weight to begin with for each phase? To gain the maximum benefits, you must use enough weight to cause you to reach failure during each set or you have not exercised all the fibers in that muscle. This is true for each phase— light, moderate, and heavy. This means your training partner would need to help you do your last repetition during each set. If you can perform more than the 5 repetitions for the heavy set, 8 for the moderate set, and 12 for the light set, you should add weight, even during a phase. Be honest with yourself, because if you fail to adjust the weight, you will not gain the strength you should be developing. Many people won't continue exercising until they reach failure and will quit before it happens. When encouraged to continue, they will say that it makes them uncomfortable to exercise to failure. If you are comfortable in the weight room, you are not training for maximum strength and could possibly have fallen into the old trap of loafing and socializing. If you are looking for comfort, don't go to a weight room and try to do a powerlifting workout.

When to Cycle

How do you know when it is time to start a cycle? This is different among lifters who have had success using varying length cycles. The length of cycles for a contest is usually between eight weeks and 16 weeks depending on how low in intensity you want to start. If you have not been training on a regular basis, I would recommend a 16-week cycle, starting with repetitions of 8 to 10 for three weeks and changing to 6 to 8 repetitions for three weeks. Then drop down to sets of 5 repetitions, and continue to raise weight and drop repetitions until you are doing doubles a week before a contest. Take a week off before the contest. If you have been training on a regular basis, you might want to start with five weeks of 5s, three weeks of 3s, and two weeks of 2s. As you learn how your body reacts, you can make adjustments on your next cycle until you have reached the combination of repetitions, sets, weight, and time that works best for you.

Sample Training Cycles

In the next pages you will find profiles of five powerlifters who train regularly. Each has developed a training program and nutritional plan that works well for him or her. What works for these lifters may not work the same for you, because everyone is different, but it is useful to read about the training styles others find successful, and some elements of their programs may apply to you. Each individual's formula varies from the others, but they all include common sense, knowledge, dedication, and patience.

Profile   # Barbara Beasley (small female, 132 pounds)

Barbara is 45 years old and has been competing in powerlifting for four and a half years. Since she started, she has won the following titles:

1. 1995 Virginia State ADFPA Assisted Champion in Open and Masters
2. 1996 Virginia State ADFPA Assisted Champion in Open and Masters
3. 1996 Virginia State AAU Champion in Open and Masters
4. 1997 ADFPA Assisted State, National, and World Masters Champion
5. 1998 AAU Assisted State and International Masters Champion
6. 1999 AAU National Assisted Masters Champion
7. 1999 AAU National and World Raw Masters Champion

Barbara was 38 when she began to lift weights and compete in bodybuilding. After three and a half years she decided to switch to powerlifting. She started in the 116-pound class and has gradually moved up to the 132-pound class with approximately the same body size. This additional muscle mass has given her the strength to be a champion. Her last world championship meet was in the Raw category (no supportive gear). Her squat numbers were greatly reduced from 220 to 175 but her deadlift and bench press were not. She now advocates raw lifting as the way to go, and will probably become a vocal proponent of this style.

Her eating habits still have some carryover from her bodybuilding days but are not nearly as rigid. Here is a typical week for Barbara:

Diet

Monday through Friday

Meal 1 Bagel, banana, and egg whites

Meal 2 Oatmeal and raisins

Meal 3 Chicken or tuna, rice or cottage cheese, and a piece of fruit or broccoli

Meal 4 Chicken, turkey, or fish, rice or baked potato, and fresh steamed vegetables or salad

On Saturday and Sunday Barbara eats anything she wants but is conscious of the quantity. She eats red meat about twice a month.

Training Program

Barbara's training programs are written by Mike Craven, owner of Mike's Olympic Gym, in Mechanicsville, Virginia. She has tried the three-, four-, and six-day training routines and finds that the four-day routine is the most effective. Barbara trains year-round but has a special five-week training routine before a meet.

Barbara starts with a percentage method leading up to 95% of her last best competition lift by the fifth week. The days she lifts are Monday (bench press), Tuesday (squats), Thursday (incline bench press), and Friday (deadlift).

Day 1

Flat bench—with shirt using percentages

Bench and dumbbell work

Shoulder work

Triceps work

Abdominal work

Calves

Day 2

Squat—with suit using percentages

Heavy abdominal work

Back work—good mornings, hyper-extensions, straight-leg deadlifts

Biceps—to balance the triceps work keeping the arm symmetrical

Day 3

Incline bench

Triceps work

Shoulder work

Heavy abdominal work

Calves

Day 4

Deadlifts—off the floor only until meet

Rack work—bar elevated to approximately knee level for lockouts

Back work—good mornings, hyper-extensions

Heavy shrugs

Biceps work

Abdominal work

Barbara plans to stay in the sport for a long time for many reasons. The first reason is for her health. She also wants to show that it is possible to be both strong and feminine. If you have seen her both in lifting gear and in dressy clothes, you would agree that she meets both criteria.

Commentary

Barbara's program, both the nutritional and training aspects, is a program that the average person could follow without a major change in his or her life.

Diet

The foods Barbara eats are simple, easy to fix, and in compliance with the USDA Food Guide Pyramid's percentages of each type of food that the average person's, as well as a strength trainer's, diet should include (see figure 6.1, on page 81). She keeps her carbohydrates high for energy to complete the workouts and eats plenty of protein, but she does not believe in the amino acid/protein supplements that are advertised by companies as the answer to strength building. You get all the protein you need by following the USDA pyramid suggestions. Save the money you would spend on supplements and use it to purchase healthful food.

Training Program

Barbara uses the percentage method of training. She starts a cycle with a low percentage of her best lift and continues to add weight until she is up to 95%. This method has been used very effectively by many lifters and particularly lifters training in Louie Simmons' Gym. A lifter normally increases by two and one half percent each week during the cycle.

Barbara uses the bench press shirt and squat suit for training throughout her cycle. This is generally not done, because in a building phase you want the muscles to improve in strength, and then when the suit and shirt are worn the assistance given improves the performance. I personally believe that the supportive gear should not be used during training—only wear it when learning to use it before a meet.

Barbara trains the calves and biceps, which have no value to a powerlifter for any of the lifts in competition. Her reason for this is that she wants to keep her body symmetrical and attractive and continues to train all areas for this purpose.

Profile

Richard Coppins (medium-size male, 220 pounds)

Rich is a 53-year-old university professor who has been training and competing for only six years. Since he started, he has won the following titles:

1. Virginia State Champion—1998 and 1999
2. Masters National USAPL Champion—1998

He started weight training after an orthopedic surgeon told him that his left knee and neck were deteriorating faster than normal because of his excessive jogging. He started training two days a week by doing the bench press, and after a short time, he wanted to learn how to squat and deadlift. After learning the value of a strong lower body, he began training four days a week.

Rich was jogging 7 miles a day five to six days a week. He is 6 feet 3 inches tall and weighed 192 pounds. He continued to gain muscle and now weighs 220 pounds. He has not had any neck or knee pain since starting a lifting program.

Rich continues to make progress from meet to meet and in the last Virginia State USAPL competition, he performed the following lifts: squat, 470; bench press, 310; and deadlift, 570.

Diet

Meal 1 8 ounces orange juice, 2 large bagels, 1 cup decaffeinated coffee

Meal 2 sandwich with low-fat turkey and low-fat cheese, apple, pretzels, diet soft drink

Meal 3 chicken, pasta or rice, large garden salad, low-fat brownies

Rich eats beef once or twice a week and Chinese food once a week.

Training Program

Rich does a four-day-per-week workout, and trains in the same sequence as meet competition: squat, bench press, and deadlift.

He trains year-round and begins a cycle 11 weeks before a meet: five weeks of 5s, three weeks of 3s, two weeks of 2s, and on Monday, before the weekend meet, he does his anticipated openers with full gear and then rests until competition day.

Day 1 (Monday)

Squats—55%, 60%, 65%, 70%, and 75% of last competition maximum, doing 5 repetitions for five weeks, then 85%, 90%, and 95% using 3 repetitions per set for three weeks, and 95% and 100% for doubles for two weeks.

Hamstring curls

Quadriceps extension

Leg presses

Abdominal work

Day 2 (Wednesday)

Flat bench press—using the same percentages described in the squats

Lat pulldowns

Seated row

Biceps work

Abdominal work

Day 3 (Friday)

Deadlift—using the same percentages described previously

Leg presses

Leg extensions

Leg curls

Day 4 (Saturday)

Bench press—several sets using lighter weight with a variety of hand placements, from very narrow to very wide

Pressdowns on lat bar

Seated row

Lat pulls

Heavy biceps

Heavy abdominal work

Commentary

Like Barbara, Richard also follows a diet and training program that any person could follow without additional financial cost, preparation time, or inconvenience to him or his family.

Diet

Rich sticks to a very simple diet that would fit into anyone's family lifestyle. When he eats, he eats a lot, and his total caloric intake during the day is high, probably around 4000. He adjusts the amount of food he eats by monitoring his weight and fat percentage. He likes to stay close to his competition weight and does not like to "diet down" to meet the requirements. He is careful about what he eats but occasionally indulges in the forbidden food area; however, he quickly returns to healthy eating habits.

Training Program

Rich is my training partner; I trained and taught him how to strength train and powerlift, and I've watched him change from a 192-pound "weakling" to a 220-pound National Champion. He has the desire to improve and continues to do so from meet to meet. He *never* misses a training session and I can set my watch by his knock on my door announcing, "It's play time." The 30-pound weight gain did not cause him to change belt size, but his upper body did change considerably causing jackets and shirts not to fit. I got an almost new leather jacket out of the deal. Rich keeps meticulous records and refers back to a month ago, a year ago, and three years ago as he charts his future in powerlifting. He reads, listens to other powerlifters, experiments with various programs during an off cycle time, adjusts his program, and continues to make constant improvements.

Profile

Dave "Slice" Weiss (small male, 132 pounds)

Dave began lifting in high school to rehabilitate a shoulder injury that occurred while wrestling. He could not return to wrestling, so he continued lifting. He says he was very fortunate that his initial training was with collegiate and teenage national champions Eric Hammer, Mike Thompson, and Paul Garman. Because of this, he learned the correct form from the beginning.

Dave began training at Mike's Olympic Gym in Mechanicsville, Virginia, and gives a lot of credit to Mike for his success and longevity by focusing on correct form and sound training principles.

Dave believes that the key to success in powerlifting and any other athletic sport lies in four areas: training, nutrition, mental focus, and genetics. The athlete has control of three of the four things mentioned, especially the first two. He says not to try to take credit for your genetics but take advantage of it. The ability to focus is the key to success. He believes that the brain is the strongest muscle in the body.

Dave has won many titles:

1. Five World Drug-Free Powerlifting Federation World Titles ('92, '93, '95, '96, and '98)

2. Two world records in the deadlift: 123-pound class (513 pounds) and 132-pound class (552 pounds)
3. Every ADFPA title possible (Worlds, Open, Collegiate, and Lifetime National, as well as USPF and ADFPA State) in 1992

Diet and Supplementation

Dave is sponsored by Marathon and Sportpharma, but he stays away from supplementation as a rule. He takes a multivitamin and multi-amino tablets. He feels that supplements are overhyped and follows a good but not too strict diet to cover all the bases. He trains at 138 to 140 pounds between meets, which is approximately 13% body fat, but he trains as low as 132 pounds, which is approximately 11% body fat.

Training Program

Dave's training principle is "keep it simple," and his programs are written by Mike Craven.

Monday

Squats
Shoulder shrugs

Tuesday

Bench press
Weighted pull-ups
Dips
Light triceps pushdowns
Heavy preacher curl

Thursday

Deadlift
Hyperextensions (very heavy, up to 180 pounds)
Leg press
Calves

Friday

Flat dumbbell chest press
Rack bench (4 inches off chest)
Light dips
Light preacher curls
Heavy triceps pushdowns
Hammer curls

Assistant exercises will vary slightly. Look for simple (one joint and one muscle) vs compound (multiple joints and muscles involved) movements and not too many movements per workout.

Commentary

Dave's nutritional habits and training plan are unique to him; he has found out what works best for him. Dave is a very dedicated lifter who gives his all at every practice.

Diet

Dave declined to give me his diet in detail. However, his philosophy is to practice moderation in eating and not to go overboard on the supplements. I have known Dave "Slice" for several years and in my opinion he would be considered a "maverick;" for the most part, he does his own thing, but it works for him. He believes in the "keep it simple" philosophy for eating as well as for his training program. Dave is another champion that leads a "normal" life as far as nutrition is concerned.

Training Program

Dave trains like a man in a trance and has complete focus on what he is doing. He does not come to the gym for a social hour and has been thought of as "unfriendly" by some that did not understand. Dave sets his goals for each meet and believes without any doubt that he can make those goals a reality. He attacks the weights and works out with the same attitude he would if he were competing for the world championships on each lift, giving his all. This intensity has always produced results and has made him one of the most successful lifters in the world.

Profile   # Kathy Roberts (large female, 198 pounds)

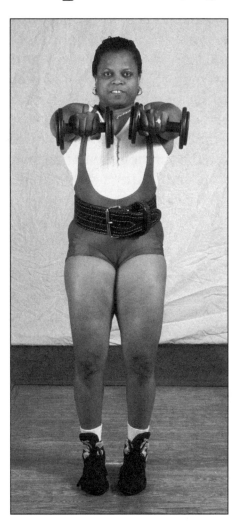

Kathy is very adamant about being "lifetime drug free." She started out as a bodybuilder but changed to power-lifting once in the gym. She started out in the 132-pound class and is presently in the 198-pound class. She has set 12 world records, 12 American records, four regional records, and 19 state records in four different weight classes.

Diet

Kathy does not eat french fries, hamburgers, milkshakes, or donuts—she considers them junk food. She does not consider what she eats a diet, but a way of life. She eats turkey sandwiches, yogurt, egg whites, applesauce, boiled chicken, vegetables, an occasional piece of steak, and lots of bananas and carbohydrates. The carbohydrates come from pastas, potatoes, and rice. She eats five or six meals throughout the day. Kathy admits that she eats a lot of food. The only supplement she takes is a multivitamin.

Training Program

Kathy trains hard all year, whether for a meet or just to get stronger. She trains four days a week, concentrating on different parts of the body each day.

Day 1

Bench press

Triceps

Day 2

Back (lat pulls, bent-over rowing, one-arm dumbbell rows)

Biceps (preacher curls, dumbbells, hammer curls, and concentration curls)

Day 3

Squat

Extensions

Flexion (leg curls)

Calves (standing and seated)

Day 4

Shoulder presses

Dumbbell work for the anterior, middle, and posterior deltoids

Triceps (pressdowns on the lat bar)

Commentary

Kathy is one of the most dedicated people I know. Her life revolves around strength, not only for herself but for other people. She is a personal trainer and motivational speaker who carries her message about drug-free strength to any interested group. She progressed from 132 pounds to 198 pounds over a 9-year period. Along the way she managed to set records at all levels in each weight class she went through. She has stabilized at 198 pounds and looks and feels good at this weight. I would not recommend this fast rate of weight gain for most people, but with Kathy's devoted lifestyle the gain was almost all usable muscle.

Training Program

Kathy trains four days a week, splitting the body into four groups and concentrating on one group each day. She trains with an intensity that completely takes over her mind and body during her training sessions. She is different than most lifters who do cycles of light, moderate, and heavy weights because she trains hard year round. This type of training is not recommended by most coaches because the body needs a change from hard training to light or moderate, giving it a change of pace. Also, most people who train the same way all the time become bored and are the ones most likely to quit. Quitting never enters Kathy's mind, and she has employed this type of training very successfully.

Profile

Kent Johnson (large male, 230 pounds)

Kent began lifting as a high school freshman after the football coach told him that he was too small. At 14 years old he weighed 135 pounds. Today he is 35 years old and 230 pounds of solid muscle.

An army officer introduced Kent to powerlifting when he was 18 years old. From that time on, he has been dedicated to the sport and has won numerous world and national championship titles. He began to lift in the 181-pound division and now lifts either in the 220- or 242-pound division.

Diet

Kent follows the nutritional plan listed here. For more information on this plan, as well as nutritional values for each item, please see page 85.

Meal 1 Frosted Mini-Wheats, 6 egg whites, 24 ounces of water

Meal 2 chicken breast, rice, apple

Meal 3 chicken breast, rice, spinach

Meal 4 turkey sandwich

Meal 5 lean sirloin steak, rice, spinach

Meal 6 peanut butter and jelly sandwich

Kent drinks 16 to 24 ounces of water with each meal.

This is a plan for a large man (230 pounds or larger). Consuming almost 3,000 calories produces a lot of energy and allows you to exercise at the high intensity level suggested in the workout plan. However, if you eat like this and don't increase your workout intensity, you will find fat creeping onto your body. Also, if you are not this big, you should adjust your calorie intake. If you are only two-thirds this size (150 pounds), then adjust the portions to two-thirds of 3,000 calories, or 1,980. Also notice the amount of water (72 ounces) that Kent suggests on this diet, which is a lot of water and will cause frequent trips to the bathroom at first. Keep in mind that muscles are composed of 70% water, and that body heat, especially during exercise, is regulated by perspiration from the skin. Never try to lose weight by restricting your water intake; this practice could lead to serious consequences.

Training Cycle

Kent has a training cycle that he used to win six national powerlifting titles, two second-place finishes in senior national meets, and an alternate position on two U.S. powerlifting teams.

Following are Kent's training percentages for both a 15-week training cycle and a 12-week training cycle. They are essentially the same, except on the 12-week cycle the first three weeks are eliminated and the lifter begins at the 57.5% level of lifting. I will give the 15-week percentages for the squat, bench press, and deadlift only; these should not be used with support work. Suggestions for support work are given later in the program.

During the first 10 weeks (or 7 weeks), the sets are for 8 repetitions each.

Week	Percentage	Week	Percentage
1	50	6	62.5
2	52.5	7	65
3	55	8	67.5
4	57.5 (start here for 12-week cycle)	9	70
5	60	10	72.5

During the last five weeks the sets are for 5 to 6 reps each.

Week	Percentage	Week	Percentage
11	75	14	82.5
12	77.5	15	85
13	80		

Kent recommends 7 to 10 days of rest to recover from this cycle before competition.

Kent has developed a way to determine how much your maximum lift will be by using a coefficient determined by the number of repetitions you did. For example, if you lifted 100 pounds 8 times, you would multiply 100 by 1.15 and your projected max would be 115 pounds. Charts such as the ones below vary according to individual. It takes much record keeping until you are able to predict the maximum amount of weight you can lift without actually performing the lift. This one works for Kent; perhaps a different system would work for you.

Squat and Deadlift

Repetitions	Multiply by	Repetitions	Multiply by
8	1.15	3	1.08
5–6	1.12	2	1.05

Bench Press

Repetitions	Multiply by	Repetitions	Multiply by
8	1.48	3	1.43
5–6	1.45	2	1.40

Training Program

When training for a competition, Kent uses the following program. He warns that this is a very strenuous program and should be used only by serious lifters.

Monday

Bench press—30% × 10 × 2, 50% × 6 × 1, 52.5% × 8 × 4, 50% to failure

Incline press—75% × 8 × 3

Decline press—75% × 8 × 3

The following are in compound sets. For example, you would do a set of the lat pulldowns and a set of the cable rows without resting, then rest and repeat until 3 sets are completed.

Lat pulldown to the front, cable rows—75-80% × 8 × 3

Shoulder dumbbell press, lat dumbbell raises—75-80% × 8 × 3

Biceps curl with straight bar, hammer curls—75-80% × 8 × 3

Closed grip bench press, triceps extension—75-80% × 8 × 3

Tuesday

Squat—30% × 10 × 2, 50% × 6 × 1, 52.5% × 8 × 4, 50% to failure

Walkouts and half squats—Done every other week

Do 3 sets of 8 reps at 100 pounds more than your workout weight. For example, if your workout weight is 250, add 100 and do half squats with 350.

The following are done for 8 reps:

Squat press—4 sets at 75-80%

Seated leg curls—3 sets at 75-80%

Prone leg curl—3 sets at 75-80%

Standing and seated calf raises—4 sets at 75-80%

Thursday

Bench press assistant exercises

All of the following are done for 8 repetitions and at 65 to 70% of your max lift:

Dumbbell press—4 sets

Incline press—3 sets

Decline press—3 sets

Shoulder press—2 sets

Lateral raises—2 sets

Biceps curls and triceps extension—3 sets (do both exercises before resting)

Friday

Deadlift—30% × 10 × 2, 50% × 6 × 1, 52.5% × 8 × 4, 50% to failure

The following exercises should be done for 8 reps at 75 to 80% max:

Shrugs—3 sets

Shoulder rolls—2 sets

Straight-leg deadlift—3 sets

Heavy lockouts (use a weight 100 pounds more than your workout weight if you weigh 220 pounds or more; less if you are a smaller person)—3 sets of 8

Cable rows, lat pulldowns (compound)—3 sets of 8 for 65-70% (both exercises without a rest period equal one set)

Saturday

Squat and deadlift assistant exercises

Kent does a very intense routine for this day, and it will take a beginner a while to work up to this point. Don't feel that you have to do everything the first cycle, but let it be your goal.

The following exercises use various percentages working up to 60 to 75% and 8 to 15 repetitions per set.

Kneeling hamstrings—8 sets

Seated leg curls—6 sets

Prone leg curls—6 sets

Leg extensions—11 sets

Hip adduction—7 sets

Hip abduction—7 sets

Standing and seated calf (compound)—7 sets

Commentary

A look at Kent's nutritional plan and training program shows you that he has put a lot of time and thought into his powerlifting. He monitors his nutrition carefully and uses a specific percentage system for training.

Diet

Kent is a big eater and has to be constantly aware of his present weight or he would gain a large number of unwanted pounds quickly. Strength trainers seem to have the desire to consume a lot of food and we don't know which comes first: a big eater who trains for strength, or a strength trainer who needs additional food to become strong. Kent is very knowledgeable about nutrition and plots his intake by adding up the amount of calories from carbohydrate, protein, and fat. He takes in 60% carbohydrates, 20-25% protein, and 15-20% fat, which is recommended by sport nutritionists familiar with strength training.

Training Program

Kent trains using a carefully arranged program of percentages that is similar to the workouts of Barbara Beasley and David Weiss, which were designed by Mike Craven. Louie Simmons, who writes a monthly article for USAPL's powerlifting magazine, is a promoter of the percentage method. Simply stated, this method starts at around 52 to 60% of your last best lift, and progresses each week by 2.5% up to 85%. At this point, you "max out" and set new percentages for another cycle. This method has proven very successful for the people who use it. Kent trains with high intensity and constantly talks to himself to get his adrenaline flowing. He developed a ritual to do this and it has proven very successful. During his off cycle he uses a system usually associated with bodybuilding, using lighter weights, higher reps, short rest periods, multiple sets, and multiple exercises for the same body part. However, when training for a meet, Kent returns to a strength building program with no problem adjusting to the change.

Now that you have read the nutritional plans and training programs of successful lifters, you realize that champion lifters are just people, a seamstress and business owner, a university professor, a personal trainer, a computer programmer, and a personal trainer and motivational speaker. These people made a decision to become strong and wanted to be the best at being stronger than other people of the same size, gender, and age. They are all happy and confident with their lives.

I profiled these five people in the hopes of dispelling any beliefs that a person must completely change his or her life in order to be a strength trainer. It's true that strength trainers must devote time, energy, and money to their training and programs, but for the most part they lead normal lives, eat normal foods, and look like other people, with the exception of additional strength and confidence. These profiles also show you that there is not just one recipe for success; each person must consider the options and tailor a nutritional and training program that best suits his or her needs.

The four-point stance in football is similar to the squat position.

Sports

So far, I have told you how to gain strength to be a good competitive powerlifter. Can you use this strength for anything else? Obviously, the answer is yes. Being strong makes everything so much easier in everyday living. It gives you added confidence, makes you feel better about yourself, and most important for young people, helps you become more successful in sports.

Let us put our imaginations to work for a moment and imagine a proper squat. Then think about this position and various positions in different sports that use the same muscles. For example, if you rotate the squat position forward, you will notice that it becomes a four-point stance used in football and a starting position for a sprint in track events. The bench press helps in pushing someone away from you while playing football, getting a position under the goal in basketball, or pushing someone away during a wrestling match. The deadlift is one of the most natural and functional moves a person can perform. However, most people do it incorrectly, which limits the amount of weight lifted and could possibly lead to an injury and a

The bench press strengthens the muscles used in wrestling.

painful back. The deadlift exercise uses most of the major muscle groups. This exercise strengthens and stabilizes the joints of the body, decreasing the possibility of injury caused by forceful contact and falls that are common in most sports. Chapter 8 provides examples of how an athlete can put together a training program using powerlifting exercises.

Summary

You have learned how to develop a detailed workout program from the examples of world and national champions, who are ordinary people with extraordinary strength. Each athlete featured in this book has taken the basics of training and nutrition and developed them into a program that fits their individual needs. The methods described in this chapter will work and they will cause you to develop more strength than you ever thought possible. This will not happen by talking about a program, thinking about a program, dreaming about a program, or watching other people do a program. You must *do* the program before it will work for you.

Proper Nutrition

Powerlifters, bodybuilders, and athletes in all sports are looking for the magic formula or combination of foods that will provide maximum energy and build fat-free muscles. Many companies claim to have the necessary supplements that will transform the average person into an outstanding athlete, bodybuilder, or powerlifter. Millions of people seeking the "secret" buy these products and expect results that match the descriptions in the ads. The greatest results from these transactions are the monetary profits that the companies make. They know that people want to believe they can buy a quick and easy way to be successful in developing great strength, large muscles, and success in sports. Strength-developing foods are probably found on your table every day; you should not waste a lot of time and money looking for the magic food. The secret is in the percentage of protein, fat, and carbohydrate consumed daily. For complete detailed information, I highly recommend the book *Power Eating* by Susan M. Kleiner and Maggie Greenwood-Robinson (Human Kinetics, 1997), which I consulted frequently when putting together this chapter.

Protein

One of the first questions I hear from a beginning weight trainer is "How much should I increase my protein now that I am on a weightlifting program?" People are very surprised when I tell them it is probably not necessary to increase their protein intake at all. They are often confused because supplement companies tell them that a large quantity of protein is necessary. This is not the answer they expect or want to hear, and they appear to be disappointed that I do not encourage massive amounts of protein. Many people have tried to convince me that I am wrong, citing information they have read in a magazine, which just happens to sell protein powder, pills, and shakes. This information is usually accompanied by pictures of people with beautiful physiques who claim that protein products are what made it all possible. I am aware that this type of advertising is a powerful tool, especially if the advertisement tells people what they want to hear and is extremely hard to counter with legitimate information that does not make big promises. I am not trying to diminish the importance of protein and amino acids for muscle development; I want to point out how protein should be used and in what amount.

Protein is found in every part of the body and is responsible for the replacement, repair, and growth of body tissue. Protein also is responsible for regulating metabolism, maintaining water balance, protecting against disease, transporting nutrients in and out of cells, transporting oxygen, and regulating blood clotting. Now that the importance of protein has been established, we must determine the correct amount of protein to consume and if there is any danger of consuming too much protein.

The recommended daily allowance (RDA) for the average person is 0.8 grams per kilogram of body weight. A kilogram is equal to 2.2 pounds, so if you want to know how many kilograms you weigh, divide your weight in pounds by 2.2. For example, if you weigh 220 pounds, you would divide by 2.2 to get 100 kilograms. You do need more protein than a sedentary person, but how much? In the book *Power Eating* by Kleiner and Greenwood-Robinson, 1.6 grams per kilogram of body weight is recommended for an active person. In the case of the 100-kilogram person, it would be 160 grams of protein each day. Kleiner and Greenwood-Robinson also recommend vegetarian strength trainers to take in as much as 2.0 grams of protein for each kilogram of body weight.

Using a high-protein diet for weight loss or muscle gain is dangerous. The low fiber content in a high-protein diet will cause digestive problems, including constipation. Excessive protein flushes calcium from the body, which leads to osteoporosis. The excess nitrogen in a high-protein diet is dangerous to the kidneys, and excess protein causes dehydration. The dehydration causes a loss in weight, leading some people to believe that this is a good way to diet, but the water returns as soon as you resume your normal diet.

Remember the 220-pound strength trainer who needed 160 grams of protein? To give you some idea about what you need to eat, for example, 4 ounces of lean beef is 24 grams of protein, one cup of low fat milk is 8 grams of protein, 2 tablespoons of peanut butter is 8 grams of protein, and one-half cup of beans is 8 grams of protein. Labels on all food packages list the amount of protein per serving.

Fat

People usually talk about fat in negative terms. Did you ever hear someone say they wanted to gain some fat? Bodybuilders avoid fat as if it were poison, and most people want to lose extra body fat. Fat in the diet is an essential element, but if you eat too much fat, you will find it accumulating around your waist, legs, and buttocks. Fat is a large source of energy for all of us. In fact, Kleiner reports that it is estimated that the average adult male has enough fat to provide the energy to ride a bike 2,000 miles. Then why isn't fat a major contributor to energy during exercise? Oxygen must be present for your body to burn fat, and it takes about 20 to 40 minutes of exercise before fat is available to the muscles as fuel. As your conditioning level increases, your body increases its ability to utilize fat as an energy source. If you are overweight and out of shape, you are less able to burn fat as a fuel, but if you are in good condition, you can burn fat very well as fuel.

The two polyunsaturated fats, linoleic acid and linolenic acid, are essential for normal growth, maintenance of cell membranes, and healthy arteries and nerves. The normal American diet contains far too much fat. How much is enough? Your diet should contain no more than 30% fat. If you want to lose fat weight, your diet should contain no more than 20% fat. A gram of fat contains nine calories, which is more than twice as many calories as a gram of carbohydrate or protein contains (each contain four calories). For example, if you consume a 2,000-calorie diet each day, 66 grams of fat would make up your fat requirement if you want to keep your fat intake at 30%. If you wanted to lose fat weight, 20% fat intake would be about 44 grams of fat.

Carbohydrates

One of the keys to being successful in strength training, bodybuilding, and other sports is the carbohydrates you eat. The average person should consume about 58% carbohydrates, but athletes, bodybuilders, and strength trainers should increase this to 70% as the intensity of training increases. Carbohydrates are the most efficient sources of energy available to the muscles. A high-carbohydrate diet gives you the energy to train harder and longer, thereby promoting muscle and strength gain. Carbohydrates are quickly broken down into glucose, which is also known as blood sugar. Blood sugar begins to circulate in the bloodstream and is available for use by the brain and the nervous system. If your brain is not getting enough blood sugar, it will have trouble controlling your muscles, causing you to feel weak and shaky. Endurance athletes have known for a long time that carbohydrate loading improves their performance in competition, but strength trainers also must learn that carbohydrates are just as important for them. It takes between 2,500 and 3,500 calories to maintain a pound of muscle, which is a lot of energy, and carbohydrates are the cleanest, most immediate sources for building these muscles. If taken in adequate amounts, carbohydrates can provide all the energy requirements, leaving protein to do the job of building and repairing muscle tissue.

You can develop your own high-carbohydrate diet by using the Food Guide Pyramid, developed by the United States Department of Agriculture, to serve as a practical tool for planning. There are six categories of food in the pyramid: (1) bread, cereal, rice, and pasta group, (2) vegetable group, (3) fruit group, (4) meat, poultry, fish, dry beans, eggs, and nuts group, (5) milk, yogurt, and cheese group, and (6) fats, oils, and sweets group. This pyramid is illustrated in figure 6.1.

What should your daily intake of carbohydrates be? If you are on a 3,500-calorie diet, 2,400 (about 70%) of those calories should come from carbohydrates. Each gram of carbohydrate contains 4 calories; therefore, you should eat about 600 grams (2,400 calories divided by 4) of carbohydrates each day.

When should you eat carbohydrates? Should you eat carbohydrates before a workout? It all depends on the type of workout you are planning to do that day. If you are planning on doing a high-intensity (high weight, low reps, short rest) workout to build maximum strength and muscle mass, you should take in carbohydrates before and during your workout. Before a workout means two to three hours before, and during means to sip a carbohydrate drink to keep you hydrated as well as energized. If you have a long workout and sip a carbohydrate drink throughout the workout, you might take in too many calories, so you should alternate drinking plain water and a carbo drink. Also immediately following an intense workout, your muscle cells will absorb glucose (carbohydrates) like a sponge and replenish themselves, which greatly reduces the

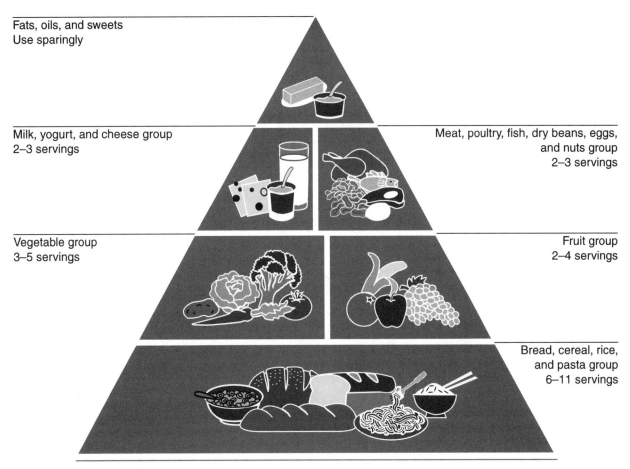

Fats, oils, and sweets
Use sparingly

Milk, yogurt, and cheese group
2–3 servings

Meat, poultry, fish, dry beans, eggs,
and nuts group
2–3 servings

Vegetable group
3–5 servings

Fruit group
2–4 servings

Bread, cereal, rice,
and pasta group
6–11 servings

Figure 6.1 USDA Food Guide Pyramid.
Source: U.S. Department of Agriculture/U.S. Department of Health and Human Services

amount of time it takes your muscles to recover and be ready for the next workout. What is the best type of carbohydrate? Carbohydrates with a high glycemic index, which is a scale describing how fast a food is converted to glucose and energy. The higher the food's glycemic index rating, the faster it will be converted to energy. Table 6.1 ranks foods according to their glycemic effect. You can see that carbohydrates from sport drinks, raisins, bananas, or potatoes are excellent choices for a quick recovery. However, you should take no more than 40 to 60 grams of high glycemic carbohydrates per hour or the body will respond negatively and lower the blood sugar level.

Many powerlifters and bodybuilders also attempt to increase the rate of muscle growth and energy level by drinking a carbohydrate supplement that contains protein. Gatorade has a product for this called GatorPro, which provides 360 calories, 59 grams of carbohydrates, 17 grams of protein, and 7 grams of fat. Kleiner and Greenwood-Robinson suggest an effective homemade version of GatorPro, which includes a packet of Carnation Instant Breakfast, 8 ounces of skim milk, 1 medium banana, and 1 tablespoon of

Table 6.1 Glycemic Index of Carbohydrate Foods*

High glycemic	Moderate glycemic	Low glycemic
Beverages Gatorade–91 Carbonated soft drink–68	**Bread and grain products** Pasta–41 Rice, white–56 Rice, brown–55 Pumpernickel bread–41 Bran muffin–60 Popcorn–55	**Bread and grain products** Barley–25 Power bar–30-35 PR bar–33
Bread and grain products Bagel–72 Bread, white–70 Bread, whole wheat–69 Corn flakes–84 Oatmeal–61 Graham crackers–74 Grape Nuts–67	**Fruits** Orange juice–57 Bananas, overripe–52 Orange–43 Apple juice, unsweetened–41	**Fruits** Apple–36 Apricots, dried–31 Bananas, underripe–30 Grapefruit–25 Pear–36 Fructose–23**
Fruits Watermelon–72 Raisins–64 Honey–73**	**Vegetables** Corn–55 Peas–48 Sweet potato–54	**Legumes** Lima beans–32 Chickpeas–33 Green beans–30 Kidney beans–27 Lentils–29 Split peas, yellow–32
Vegetables Potato, baked–85 Potato, microwaved–82	**Legumes** Baked beans–48 Lentil soup–44	**Dairy products** Chocolate milk–34 Skim milk–32 Whole milk–27 Yogurt, low fat, with fruit–33

*Index based on 50 grams of carbohydrate per serving.
**Not nutritionally equivalent to fruit.

peanut butter. Blend until smooth. This provides you with 438 calories, 17 grams of protein, 70 grams of carbohydrate, and 10 grams of fat. The protein and carbohydrates in this drink trigger the release of insulin and growth hormone in your body. Insulin helps carry the amino acids into the cells, reassembles those amino acids into body tissue, and prevents muscle wasting and tissue loss. The growth hormone increases the rate of protein production in the body, which encourages muscle-building activity and promotes fat burning.

Some people promote low-carbohydrate diets for quick weight loss. However, the weight you lose is water and muscle and very little fat. This is one of the least desirable ways to lose weight. If carbohydrates are severely restricted, the body will begin to use proteins as a source of energy. This process is actually taking muscle tissue and converting it to energy; in other words, the body is forced to reduce the size and strength of the muscles to provide energy for workouts. If this is the case the long, hard workouts are actually working against you and the improvements you want.

Eating Guidelines

How many calories do you need? How can you determine what is right for you? Here is a formula that is generally accepted by most researchers and nutritionists. If you are a woman, multiply your body weight (in pounds) by 8, which will give you the number of calories necessary to keep your body functioning—your lungs, heart, digestive system, and so on. For example, 120 pounds multiplied by 8 gives you 960 calories. Now add 400 or 500 for daily activities, which is now approximately 1,400 calories. If you are doing high-intensity training, you should add another 250 to 400 for each hour you are training and now you are up to or over 2,000 calories each day. You should remember that this is only a general guide. If you are losing weight, you should increase your daily caloric intake, and if you are gaining fat, reduce the number of daily calories.

Your caloric needs are not the same throughout your cycle or training program. For example, during your building phase, you should consume between 50 and 60 calories per kilogram of body weight. For a 220-pound/100 kilogram person, the total daily calories would be between 5,000 and 6,000 per day. This is a lot of calories and should be attained by slowly adding a few hundred calories each day until you have reached the desired level of muscle but are not gaining fat. Keep a close check on your progress, and adjust your consumption accordingly.

General Sample Diet

The sample diet shown at left, taken from *Power Eating* by Kleiner and Greenwood-Robinson, is for a 180-pound man, and it consists of 4,250 calories. Refer to Kleiner's

Breakfast	Kleiner's muscle-building formula 6 pancakes, 4 inches round 3 tablespoons syrup 1 cup orange juice
Snack	1 serving high-carbohydrate replacer 1 cup low-fat yogurt
Lunch	1 piece pita bread, 6 inches round, stuffed with 3 ounces of low-fat cheese, sprouts, sliced tomato, sliced red pepper, 1/8 avocado, 1 tablespoon nonfat ranch dressing carrot sticks 1 large pear 1 cup of skim milk
Snack	1 serving high-carbohydrate replacer 2 granola bars 8 dried apricot halves
Workout	40 ounces carbohydrate-electrolyte replacer
After workout	meal replacer
Dinner	3 cups stir-fried vegetables with 1/2 pound tofu 1 tablespoon oil 1 cup brown rice 2/3 cup fat-free frozen yogurt with 1 cup raspberries

recipe on pages 81-82, which is referred to as "Kleiner's muscle-building formula" in the sample diet.

For various reasons, you might have to deviate from this diet, such as nonavailability of products and allergies, but if a replacement is made, be sure it is from the same food group (see figure 6.1 on page 81). Also, you should make adjustments to the number of calories suggested based on your own body weight. If you weigh only 132 pounds, you would drastically reduce the amount of food because you do not need that many calories for energy, and the amounts given here would result in an accumulation of unwanted fat. On the other extreme, if you weigh more than 180 pounds, you would need to increase the amount of food to supply the calories necessary for strenuous workouts. You would have to experiment with the amount of food and calories needed to supply the required energy for your workout.

Sample Diet for Gaining Weight

If you have decided to gain a half-pound of muscle each week, you will need to consume an additional 1,800 calories each week, or 260 additional calories each day. What does that mean in terms of everyday food? I will give a few examples, but complete lists of the caloric content of all foods, as well as fast foods, are available almost anywhere, or if all else fails, become a label reader when you shop for groceries. Look for a product that contains 60 to 65% carbohydrates, has no more than 20% fat, and contains at least 15% protein. Following are some examples.

Food	Calories
Apple	81
Banana	109
Whole wheat bread, 2 slices	138
Bagel, plain	195
Oatmeal	104
Baked potato, with skin	206
Navy beans, 1 cup	296

As you can see from this list, you could eat a bagel and an apple every day in addition to your current meal plan and you would be eating an additional 1,932 calories per week—more than enough for the desired weight gain. Pick foods that are healthy, provide energy, taste good, and are easy to carry around in your workout bag or backpack to snack on during the day.

Sample Diet for Losing Fat and Gaining Muscle

The following is a nutritional plan used by Kent Johnson, a world record holder and a multi-year national champion. This diet plan is also featured in chapter 5 along with his workout program.

You will notice that he eats less than most of the plans listed here (3,000 calories a day) and still has energy for intense exercise. This could be puzzling or appear to contradict previous plans; however, there is a reason for this. I have known Kent for seven years and I know that he loves to eat and has a tendency to gain weight when he is not in training for a meet. This weight gain is in the form of fat, while his muscles become somewhat smaller than they were in peak condition. It is not unusual for strong people to enjoy eating and sometimes they eat more than they should. This diet is designed to

Kent Johnson's Nutritional Plan

Time	Source	Calories	Protein (g)	Fat (g)	Carbohydrates (g)
7:00 A.M.	1 cup Frosted Mini-Wheats	408	12	1	94
	6 egg whites	78	16	0	2
	24 oz water				
9:30 A.M.	4 oz chicken breast	180	35	4	0
	1 cup rice	248	4.5	0.3	55
	1 apple (3 oz)	48	0.2	0.3	13
	16 oz water				
12:30 P.M.	4 oz chicken breast	180	35	4	0
	1 cup rice	248	4.5	0.3	55
	1/2 cup spinach	28	3.5	0.3	4
	16 oz water				
3:30 P.M.	turkey sandwich	277	33.9	4.2	32.9
	16 oz water				
7:00 P.M.	8 oz sirloin steak (lean)	456	65	20	0
	1 cup rice	248	4.5	0.3	55
	1/2 cup spinach	28	3.5	0.3	4
	16 oz water				
11:00 P.M.	peanut butter and jelly sandwich	487	20	23.5	49
Total		2914	237.6	58.5	363.9

provide energy as well as the required ingredients to build muscle and strength. Kent loses a few pounds on this diet during the 12-week program, and the weight loss is primarily in the form of fat (his total body fat starts at 18 to 20% and decreases to 10 to 12%). He carefully monitors his weight, percentage of body fat, and strength. If his training program shows signs of not improving at the expected rate, he increases his calorie intake.

Sample Diet for an Older Medium-Size Male

The following (on page 87) is a nutritional plan that I use during the 10- to 14-week training cycle. I am 63 years old, 5 feet 7 inches tall, and my weight varies from 192 to 202 pounds. I have found that as I age, I am unable to eat as much food as I used to without gaining fat. Therefore, this nutritional plan will appear to be limited in calories. I also "eat to the workout," which means that when I have a lower-body workout I eat more than if I were taking a day off or doing the bench press. I particularly watch my intake over the weekend when I have the urge to overeat and eat the wrong foods. I also try not to inconvenience my family by demanding meals that are difficult to prepare.

You will notice that I drink a lot of milk and orange juice. I grew up drinking a lot of milk and eating red meat. Since I began studying nutrition, I have changed from whole milk to skim milk and lean red meat. Most normal diets provide the required nutrients to achieve and maintain strength if you eat the proper amounts. If you eat more than is required for your workout intensity, you will gain unwanted fat.

Things I Nibble On

> Hard pretzels
>
> Dried fruit
>
> Hard candy

On special occasions (Thanksgiving, Christmas, and parties), I eat whatever is there and make adjustments the next day to balance the extra calories.

I drink water all day. I always have my bottle close during work or workouts, and I make sure that I get the required 64 ounces each day. I will drink more water when drinking from a bottle than from a water fountain, even though the fountain is handy. I can easily monitor the amount of water I drink by counting the number of times I fill my 17-ounce bottle.

Monday

Breakfast	Morning snack	Lunch	Afternoon snack	Dinner
Oatmeal 2 pieces toast 8 oz skim milk 8 oz orange juice	1 bagel or piece of fruit	Cottage cheese and peaches Bagel	Large apple or banana	Grilled steak Mashed potato Green beans Green salad with low-fat dressing

Tuesday

Breakfast	Morning snack	Lunch	Afternoon snack	Dinner
Cold cereal 1 banana 8 oz orange juice	1 bagel or piece of fruit	Sub sandwich (no mayonnaise)	Large apple or banana	Homemade soup Crackers Tossed salad

Wednesday

Breakfast	Morning snack	Lunch	Afternoon snack	Dinner
2 pieces French toast with syrup 8 oz skim milk 8 oz orange juice	1 bagel or piece of fruit	Large bowl of soup Crackers or bagel	Large apple or banana	Baked chicken Baked potato Pork and beans 2 slices whole wheat bread Tossed salad

Thursday

Breakfast	Morning snack	Lunch	Afternoon snack	Dinner
2 soft-boiled eggs 2 pieces toast 8 oz skim milk 8 oz orange juice	1 bagel or piece of fruit	Sub sandwich (no mayonnaise)	Large apple or banana	Hamburger patty Green vegetable Large fruit salad 2 slices whole wheat bread 2 scoops of ice cream

Friday

Breakfast	Morning snack	Lunch	Afternoon snack	Dinner
Oatmeal 2 pieces toast 8 oz skim milk 8 oz orange juice	1 bagel or piece of fruit	Cottage cheese and peaches Bagel	Large apple or banana	1/2 broiled seafood platter 1/2 baked potato Tossed salad

Saturday

Breakfast	Morning snack	Lunch	Afternoon snack	Dinner
Cold cereal Fruit 8 oz orange juice	1 bagel or piece of fruit	Large bowl of homemade soup Crackers or bagel 2 scoops of ice cream	Large apple or banana	Baked pork chop Mashed potato Green beans Tossed salad 2 slices bread 2 scoops of ice cream

Sunday

Breakfast	Morning snack	Lunch	Afternoon snack	Dinner
2 large pancakes with syrup 1 egg 8 oz orange juice 8 oz milk	1 bagel or piece of fruit	Ham sandwich Bowl of tomato soup	Large apple or banana	Grilled steak Baked potato Tossed salad Pork and beans 2 slices bread

What to Eat Before a Meet

Most meets start in the mornings around 9:30 or 10:00 A.M. with the weigh-in usually from 7:00 until 8:30 A.M. Deciding what to eat after a weigh-in is an important decision for both your energy and comfort. You need a high-energy meal with little bulk, such as waffles or pancakes with plenty of syrup, and a glass of orange juice.

This is not the time to eat high-fiber meals because of the gastric upset and gas-producing effects. This would leave you bloated and uncomfortable during the competition when you tighten your belt for a lift.

What to Eat During a Meet

Continue to eat high-calorie, low-fiber snacks throughout a competition to keep your energy level high. This type of eating also produces the positive mental attitude that is so important during a meet. Foods such as brownies, bagels, peanut butter and jelly sandwiches, along with a high-carbohydrate drink, will keep the energy level high. You should eat small snacks throughout the day instead of a large meal. A large meal will cause the blood sugar level to rise and remain elevated for a short period of time and then begin to drop, causing the energy level to drop while you still have some lifts to perform. Small snacks will keep the energy level constantly high.

What to Eat After a Meet

After your last lift is completed and the meet is over, you feel relieved and begin to relax regardless of the outcome of the meet. After a short time relaxing, you suddenly realize that you are hungry for a complete meal with all the fixings. You either go home, or to your favorite restaurant, with a big appetite. The question is, what is the best kind of meal to eat to recover from the meet, restore energy, replace valuable nutrients lost during the meet, replace proteins needed to repair damaged muscles, replace calcium for bones, and so on?

There are three things you need to replace after a meet: carbohydrates, protein, and fluid. Breads, cereals, rice, pasta, all types of vegetables, and all types of fruit are excellent carbohydrate replacers. If you are a meat eater, this is the time to indulge. Meat is an excellent source of protein, which restores the amino acids lost in the destruction of muscle tissue during the competition. Make sure it is a lean cut of meat. If you are a vegetarian, eat an ample supply of rice, beans, corn, and various types of seeds. Fluids can be replaced many different ways: plain water, iced tea, sport drinks, and milk. Milk, along with other dairy products, is a source of calcium needed for bone repair.

Fluids

The extreme importance of water for a healthy body cannot be emphasized enough. Without fluids, you would die within a week. Water makes up 60 to 70% of adult body weight. How much depends on the amount of muscle mass a person has, because muscle is about 70% water, while fat is only about 15%. Water is the most abundant nutrient in the body, the medium by which all life-giving chemical reactions take place in your body. Water carries food and oxygen throughout the body and eliminates waste products. It cools you when you are hot and lubricates your joints to keep you moving.

Although almost all foods contain water, which is absorbed during digestion, it is still not enough for the healthy body. Fruits and vegetables contain 75% to 90% water, meat contains 50% to 70% water, and juice and milk contain about 85% water, which yields between 3 to 5 cups of water from food in the normal diet. But that is not enough to keep the body healthy. You need a minimum of 8 to 10 cups of pure water daily, and more if you are exercising. Monitor your fluid needs by checking your urine, which should be light-colored or clear and almost odorless; weighing yourself before and after exercise; and drinking water until you return to pre-exercise weight. Muscle cramps, burning sensations in the stomach, and a sore throat usually are signs of dehydration.

Summary

You now know the nutritional aspects of training. The best diet is like the best training program: it is tailored to each person. Although different nutritional plans are suggested depending on your size, situation, and gender, you should make the final decision by staying aware of what is happening to your body and making the necessary adjustments. Record everything you eat for a period of time while keeping records of your weight and body fat percentage. If your weight increases but your fat percentage decreases, you can be sure you are gaining muscle. However, if you gain weight and your fat percentage increases, you can be sure you are gaining fat. You don't have to eat strange, bad-tasting foods with the attitude that if it tastes good, it must be bad for you. Common sense and education are the keys to developing a nutritional plan that is delicious and good for you.

7

Lifting Ergogenics

Now you know how to train right, eat right, and rest properly to be a winner. So, it is just a matter of signing up for the meet, participating, accepting the trophy at the end of the meet, and finding room for another trophy on your mantel, right? Wrong, because everyone at the meet follows the same rules you do and there is only one first-place trophy. Why do some people seem to respond to training better than others and win?

The answers to this question revolve around what we call *lifting ergogenics*—eating, training, supplements, and supportive gear. Ergogenic substances and aids are nutritional and pharmacological agents used to enhance physical performance. Supportive gear consists of any clothes, belts, or wraps that support or enhance physical performance.

Some people have no idea why certain things are supposed to work but still blindly follow the advice of other lifters, trainers, or coaches. There are also people who have read the research and attended clinics, and they know what really works and what is myth and hype. Then there are the people who are trying to sell you something that will supposedly improve your training and performance in competition. These retailers are interested in your money and not you. So what really works and how can you tell the difference between what works and what doesn't? I will report the latest research on supplements and supportive gear. The correct diet is discussed in great detail in chapter 6 and training programs are discussed in chapter 8.

Supplements

Every supplement manufacturer guarantees that they have the product for you. But you know that you can't possibly consume or afford all the things that the retailers want you to buy. Scientists have begun to look at the nutritional requirements of muscle building. They are discovering that you can achieve amazing results from healthy products; you do not have to resort to illegal products such as steroids. In most cases if you are eating enough calories from the proper food groups, you are fulfilling your nutritional needs. However, you might want to add certain vitamins and minerals to your daily intake as a precaution against deficiency. A good antioxidant containing 100% of the recommended daily values for vitamins and minerals usually satisfies your nutritional needs.

Antioxidants

There is a lot of research published about the need for antioxidants: beta carotene (vitamin A), vitamin C, and vitamin E, as well as minerals: selenium, copper, zinc, and manganese. Antioxidants help fight *free radicals*, which are produced by the body on a daily basis. Free radicals can cause your body to age prematurely, develop cancer, cardiovascular disease, and degenerative diseases such as arthritis. Environmental factors such as cigarette smoke, vehicle exhaust fumes, radiation, excessive sunlight, and stress increase the amount of free radicals in the body. Exercise also increases free radicals, especially during such actions as heavy weightlifting or downhill running.

Vitamins

Vitamins are organic substances that are essential to normal functioning of the human body. Although vitamins do not contain caloric energy to be used by the body, these substances are essential in metabolism of fats, carbohydrates, and protein.

Vitamin E

Vitamin E seems to be one of the most successful fighters of free radicals caused by exercise. Vitamin E is found in muscle cell membranes. Dr. William Evans of Penn State studied males 30 and younger and 55 and older using 800 individual units (IU) of vitamin E per day and found that free radicals were greatly reduced. Dr. Evans also stated that 400 IU per day is sufficient in most cases, but that older people have a greater need for vitamin E and should increase their intake slightly as they age.

Vitamin C and Beta Carotene

The recommended amounts of vitamin C and beta carotene are present in the normal diet. If you follow the U.S. Department of Agriculture's Food Guide Pyramid (see page 81) and eat at least three to five servings of vegetables and two to four servings of fruits daily, you will get the recommended dose of antioxidants.

B-Complex

There are eight major B-complex vitamins that aid proper digestion, muscle contraction, and energy production.

1. Thiamin helps in releasing energy from carbohydrates. If you are eating a well-balanced, high-carbohydrate diet, you will get all the thiamin you need.

2. Riboflavin helps release energy from foods. Dairy products, poultry, fish, and grains as well as enriched and fortified cereals are rich in riboflavin, but check to see if your multiple vitamin contains 100% of the daily requirement.

3. Niacin helps release energy from foods. Lean meats, poultry, fish, and wheat germ are the best sources of niacin. A good multiple vitamin will eliminate any possible deficiencies of niacin.

4. B-12 works with folic acid to form red blood cells in the bone marrow. B-12 is the only vitamin found in animal products. If you are a vegetarian, supplement your diet with a multiple vitamin.

5. Folic acid works with B-12 to form red blood cells in the bone marrow. This vitamin is mainly found in green leafy vegetables, legumes, and whole grains. Folic acid helps cells that reproduce to synthesize proteins and nucleic acids. It is particularly important for pregnant women to get sufficient folic acid in their diets. Folic acid recently has been linked to playing a protective role in preventing cancer and heart disease. Alcohol consumption, disease, and stress will increase your need for folic acid. A multiple vitamin usually has the proper amount of this vitamin.

6. Pyridoxine, also known as B-6, is required to metabolize protein and form red blood cells. It also is essential for the healthy functioning of the brain. This vitamin comes from chicken, fish, eggs, brown rice, soybeans, oats, and whole wheat. You are probably

getting enough B-6 in a normal diet and there is no need to supplement. Also be aware that large doses can cause nerve damage.

7. Pantothenic acid aids in releasing energy from carbohydrates, fats, and protein. Pantothenic acid comes from meats, whole grains, and legumes. Adequate amounts are usually obtained from a normal daily diet.

8. Biotin is involved in fat and carbohydrate metabolism. This vitamin is found in egg yolks, soy flour, and cereals. This vitamin, along with others, is promoted as a fat burner, but no credible research has produced evidence to support this. If you are in the habit of drinking a raw egg milkshake, be aware that raw egg white contains the protein avidin, which binds with biotin in the intestine and prevents its absorption, thereby leading to a biotin deficiency.

Electrolytes

The two chief electrolytes are sodium and potassium. Sodium regulates fluid balance outside cells, while potassium regulates fluid balance inside the cells. Sodium comes from salt in the diet; most Americans eat about 2 to 3 teaspoons of salt daily, which is more than people need. You should consume no more than 1½ teaspoons of salt daily. Potassium maintains a regular heartbeat, helps muscles contract, regulates blood pressure, and transfers nutrients to cells. Potassium is not easily conserved and must be replaced by eating potassium-rich foods, such as bananas, oranges, and potatoes. If you use diuretics, you are possibly flushing potassium and other electrolytes from the body and creating a life-threatening mineral imbalance.

Minerals

Minerals are inorganic molecules that serve a variety of functions in the human body. The minerals that appear in the largest quantities—calcium, phosphorus, potassium, sulfur, sodium, chloride, and magnesium—are often called macrominerals. Other minerals are also essential to normal functioning of the body, but because they exist in smaller quantities, they are called microminerals.

Calcium

Your bones and teeth store 99% of the calcium you consume, and the remaining 1% is stored in your blood and soft tissues. Exercise increases your body's ability to absorb calcium for conducting nerve impulses, helping muscles to contract and carrying nutrients in and out of cells. The main source of calcium is from dairy products. If you don't consume enough calcium, the body will begin to take calcium from the bones and teeth, causing them to become brittle. This is especially true of women. Add dairy products to your diet to help keep your bones strong and healthy.

Iron

Strength training and aerobic training tear down muscle tissue. The body immediately sets about to rebuild this tissue, creating a need for iron. Iron combines with protein and copper to produce *hemoglobin*, which carries oxygen in the blood from the lungs to the tissues. Iron is also necessary to form *myoglobin*, which is necessary for a chemical reaction that makes muscles contract. When you have an iron deficiency you will also have an oxygen deficiency in the muscles. The best sources of iron are organ meats of animals, lean meats, and oysters. You only need about 15 milligrams of iron daily.

Zinc

Zinc is also an antioxidant that helps maintain normal taste and smell, regulates growth, and promotes wound healing. Zinc comes from meat, eggs, seafood, and whole grains. If you restrict your meat intake, take a multiple vitamin to be sure you have enough zinc.

Magnesium

Magnesium is associated with over 400 metabolic reactions and has been promoted as an aid for exercise and muscle strength. Research has not conclusively proven the link between magnesium and muscle strength and should be viewed as questionable until further research is done. The best sources of magnesium are nuts, legumes, whole grains, dark green vegetables, and seafood. If you are following a good diet plan, your daily requirements will be satisfied, and if you are taking a multiple vitamin, make sure it is formulated with 100% of the daily magnesium requirement.

Aspartate

Aspartate is mainly associated with endurance. If you do aerobics in addition to your strength training program, you should use aspartate. You can find this mineral supplement in health food stores and sports fitness centers. Aspartate turns excess ammonia caused by exercise into urea, which is then eliminated from the body through urination.

Chromium Picolinate

Chromium picolinate, a mixture of chromium and picolinic acid, has been promoted as a safe alternative to steroids as a muscle builder. However, research on its muscle-building ability is inconclusive. A word of caution about picolinic acid is that it alters the shape of cells and interferes with the function of other trace minerals and iron in the body.

When you buy supplements, use the same guidelines you use when buying your food. Buy name brands from well-established companies, not from fly-by-night companies who try to give you deals you can't refuse. You never know what is or is not in their products.

Other Supplement Sources

Try to get what you need from food through a well-planned diet. Don't fall into the habit of taking handfuls of pills and thinking they will do the same job as nutrients from food. Also, you need the calories from food if you are to be successful in muscle building and strength development. However, there are some other sources you can use to supplement your diet.

High-Carbohydrate Bar

A high-carbo bar does exactly what it says it will do—give you lots of carbohydrates. There are a lot of calories in a small bar along with other vitamins and minerals. A Power Bar contains 230 calories with only 22 calories from fat and 40 calories from protein, which means there are 168 calories from carbohydrates. The calories from the carbohydrates are what you will use to complete your workout or a competition. These calories are very usable in a short time and will not overload your stomach with bulk. However, these bars are expensive, costing around $1.50 per bar. You can get the same benefits from a bagel, and you can buy approximately five bagels for the price of one bar.

Sport Drinks

Sport drinks have become a way of life for people who participate in bodybuilding, weight training, marathon running, or any other high-intensity sport. It is common to see athletes take a Gatorade break on the sidelines or while running a marathon. Manufacturers of sport drinks emphasize the body's need to restore carbohydrates and electrolytes during intense exercise. This claim is true, but what manufacturers don't tell you is that during an intense workout, it is most important to replace water that is lost during perspiration, not carbohydrates and electrolytes. Water is also best to return the body to a normal temperature range. If the liquid you drink contains sugar or electrolytes, it must go through the digestive tract before being used to cool the body. However, if the exercise session is to last for over two hours, you should use a drink with electrolyte replacements. Also, after an extended intense exercise session, continue to consume these drinks until you weigh almost the same as you weighed before the exercise session.

Pure Oxygen

The use of pure oxygen during exercise or competition became popular after the Japanese swimming teams used it during the 1964 Olympics and defeated all other teams. These performances were attributed to the use of oxygen; therefore, coaches and trainers in all sports began to keep oxygen tanks on the sidelines for their athletes. However, after a time research showed that using oxygen and compressed air provided only a psychological boost, or placebo effect, which caused the improved performance. Air is about 21% oxygen when we breathe it in. When the average person exhales, the air is still about 16% oxygen. Therefore, we are only using a small portion of the oxygen that we breathe in. If more oxygen was needed, the muscles would just extract more from the blood.

Steroids

Steroid abuse in sports has been studied and discussed for many years. It is a way of life in some sports, and although there are concentrated efforts to eliminate use, it is still prevalent in body-building and strength sports. Steroids do promote an increase in muscle mass and strength, but the negative side effects greatly outweigh the positive results. The negative side effects of steroids include long-term illness such as heart disease, liver damage, urinary tract abnormalities, and sexual dysfunction. Short-term side effects include increased blood pressure, acne, testicular atrophy, gynecomastia, sore nipples, decreased sperm count, prostatic enlargement, increased appetite, hair loss, fever, nausea, diarrhea, nosebleeds, lymph node swelling, and a burning sensation during urination. The major psychological symptoms include paranoia, delusions of grandeur, and auditory hallucinations. The most serious side effect of anabolic steroid use is the increased probability of developing coronary artery disease.

Equipment and Clothing

The use of performance-enhancing equipment and clothing is a must if you intend to compete. Some common items are belts, body suits, bench press shirts, and wrist and knee wraps.

Lifting Belt

The lifting belt is as much a part of the weight room as the weights. It is a valuable piece of equipment for serious lifters. The function of the weight belt is to support the abdominal muscles so that they can support the back during a heavy lift. You should wear a belt for all overhead lifts, deadlifts, or squats and when the weight is more than 60% of your maximum lift. Your belt should be snug so that the abdominals will have something to press against, but not tight enough to restrict your breathing. Having your belt extremely tight does not increase your lifting ability. Your belt should only be tight for short periods, because the blood pressure is greatly elevated while the waist is constricted. This constriction makes it difficult for the blood to return to the heart from the lower body. Use your belt when appropriate but do not wear it just to look good.

Squat Suit

The squat suit is a very tight-fitting suit that covers approximately half of your thigh and proceeds past your hips and lower back, with shoulder straps to pull in place when attempting a heavy lift. There are various brands that claim to give tremendous boost to your squat, which I believe to be true. The trick is to find a suit that is right for you; otherwise, it will only be a hindrance when you are attempting your squat. The suit should be tight enough that it will take you approximately 20 minutes to put on. The suit's legs should fit snugly a little more than halfway past your knees and not pull up past this point. However, the seat should be fitted well around the buttocks with no slack at all. The shoulder straps should be tight enough that it takes another person to pull them up over your shoulders. After pulling the shoulder straps up, you should feel like you are sitting in a slingshot. When you attempt to squat without weight you will find it difficult to go down to the proper depth. A properly fitted suit gives added confidence during your lift because of the feeling of support and lift.

Deadlift Suit

The deadlift suit was devised later than the squat suit and is not used by all lifters at this time. Some lifters say that the suit works well, while others doubt the value of it. The fabric in a deadlift suit is sewn differently than in a squat suit. In a squat suit, the fabric is sewn so that the suit binds the muscles together by pulling tightly around the body, whereas the deadlift suit is sewn so that it pulls up and down the body in order to straighten the back when lifting. Again, this is something you have to experiment with to see if it helps you.

Bench Press Shirt

The bench press shirt, whether it is a pull-on or zip-up type, is an uncomfortable supportive piece of equipment. However, its value is undisputed among lifters who lift very heavy weights. It is valuable not only in adding to your lifts but in reducing the incidence of serious injury to the chest muscles (pectorals). You should practice enough in your shirt so that it works for you and not against you. This takes some time and should not be taken lightly.

Bench press shirts are made from two types of material: a spring material or a nonspring (denim) material. Before choosing which type is best for you, try a friend's shirt, talk to other lifters, read the ads, and observe which types of shirts the bench press champions use. You will own many bench press shirts before your powerlifting days are over and you will probably change brands, types, and sizes along the way.

Erector Shirt

The erector shirt is to help keep your back and torso erect while attempting a squat or deadlift. Although it resembles the bench press shirt and is put on the same way, there are big differences in what the two will do. The erector shirt has short sleeves because you do not need support for the arms while lifting. The fabric is sewn to keep your shoulders pulled back and your chest up and out, which is the desired position for both the squat and deadlift.

Squatting Briefs

Squatting briefs are used to reinforce the squat suit in the gluteal area. They are very tight and give a lot of support during the deepest part of your squat, when support is usually needed the most. They are very uncomfortable to wear but when the weight is on your back and you need all the support you can get, you are glad you have them on. (Note: Squat briefs are not legal in some organizations. The rationale for making squat briefs illegal is not very clear. Some officials argue that squat briefs give too much support. This argument seems inconsistent, as most of the other support gear gives as much or more support than squat briefs.)

Wrist Wraps

Wrist wraps are used for support during the bench press and squat. They keep the wrists from hyperextending (bending backward). Allowing the wrist to bend backward past a straight line is poor technique and can cause problems such as painful arthritis and tendinitis. You should learn to use your wrist wraps properly and always use them with heavy weights. Make sure you take your thumb out of the thumb loop before you attempt your lift.

Knee Wraps

Knee wraps are used to support the knees during a squat. They should only be used during very heavy lifting in your training program and competition. They not only provide lateral support while squatting; they provide some bounce at the bottom of the lift. This bounce at the bottom of the lift is one of the causes of knee injuries. The fabric wads up in the bend of the knees as you squat and provides the bounce you get at the bottom, but this also has a prying effect on the front of the knee that could cause injuries if used too much. Like the belt, knee wraps are used by almost all serious lifters and are an essential piece of gear for heavy lifters.

Mouth Guards

Mouth guards are used to protect the teeth during a strenuous lift. Many lifters clamp their jaws and grind their teeth while lifting. Continual teeth grinding over a period of years causes the teeth to erode if protection is not used. Mouth guards are made from rubber or plastic and are very inexpensive. They are usually fitted over the upper jaw only; however, there are models that fit over both the upper and lower jaws. Experimenting with different mouth guards will determine if you want to use them or what model to wear if you choose to use them.

Footwear

What shoes should you wear for each event? When you attend a powerlifting meet, you will see everything from combat boots to house slippers. The kind of shoes you wear for the bench press is not important as long as they are legal. You should use different shoes for the squat and deadlift.

During the squat, you need support for the ankles. Select shoes that will not slip if you take a wide stance. Some squat shoes have a heel or raised area in the back, which some lifters think will help while doing the squat. However, some lifters prefer a flat shoe because they think a heel would shift them forward, putting pressure on the lower back and quadriceps. You should experiment and use what feels best for you.

Many lifters perform the deadlift in flat-heeled shoes such as wrestling shoes, and others use slippers. The idea is to be as low to the platform as possible; therefore, the least amount of distance you have to pull the weight, the better. If you use a sumo stance, make sure your shoes do not have baby powder or some other slippery substance on them, or you will begin to slide out toward the weights, putting you in an awkward stance or near split.

Ammonia

Ammonia is used to make you more alert and concentrated so that you can focus better on the weight. A whiff of ammonia certainly gives a shock to the system, especially if you are not accustomed to using it. Whether this really helps has not been proven by research. Many people think that ammonia is like other stimulants: it takes more and more to get the desired results, until you are taking so much so frequently it could become dangerous. Ammonia should be used sparingly and with caution if you do choose to use it, and you should monitor how much and how often you are using it.

Liniment and Balms

The odors coming from a powerlifting meet are liniment, balms, and baby powder. Liniment and balms are skin irritants that cause blood to come to the surface of the skin. This extra circulation causes the muscles around the site to receive more blood. It is similar in effect to warming up using light weights and high reps. Used in combination with high repetitions, the area is warmed up and ready to go for a maximum effort with less chance of injury. Also, when used properly after strenuous exercise, liniment and balms seem to reduce soreness.

Summary

There are many products on the market that claim to improve your lifting performances. With information taken from unbiased research and scientific information, personal experiences, and testimonies from other lifters, this chapter gives you suggestions on what to use and what not to use. There are those who will disagree with these recommendations, based on their experiences and experiences of others but without scientific backing. In many cases people want to believe that something helps and will convince themselves it does, just because someone said so. If you want to experiment with anything legal, give it a try and be honest with yourself as to whether it really works.

Training Programs

All powerlifters have at least one thing in common: they all want to become stronger in the fastest and most efficient way. Powerlifting programs and schedules vary widely, depending on such variables as experience, age, commitment, gender, and genetics. Unfortunately, many of the programs offered in magazine articles represent the methods of the person presenting the program. Also, many long-term powerlifters forget the basic needs and views of those just starting; they offer advice to beginners that is more suitable to lifters with two or more years of experience in both training and competition.

Experienced powerlifters have learned, through years of training, what works best for them. They know which exercises have helped them and which exercises have not. They know when to work through pain and when to back off and rest a painful area. The programs they use and the schedules and goals they set reflect this experience.

Older powerlifters may have gray or thinning hair, wrinkles, glasses, or hearing aids. However, none of these conditions adversely affects the muscles or the strength-gaining capacity of the muscles. Their worst problem is the well-meaning people who tell them to take it easy and make excuses for them when they fail. People are told that it takes elderly people (whatever that age is) longer to recover from a set, workout, and injury. However, this is true only if you are not conditioned for a hard workout. This is also true for poorly conditioned young people—it has nothing to do with age. These myths are built on lack of knowledge about the capabilities of elderly people. Personal trainers and doctors usually play it safe and tell their clients and patients what they have heard other people say—to take it easy. All the recent research indicates that muscle tissue of older people responds the same to training as muscle tissue of young people. Also, injured muscle tissue in an older person will heal at the same rate as muscle tissue in a younger person if the treatment and rehabilitation are the same. We should quit babying elderly people and encourage them to push their limits. Don't caution them any more than you would caution a young person. Who decides the point in a person's life when they become elderly? Is it 40, 50, 60, or what? We have all seen 40-year-olds who look and act old, and we have seen 70-year-olds who look and act young. If a person's only "disease" is age, that person should not be encouraged to take it easy. If you are in this category and people try to get you to slow down, stay away from them. Although these people mean well, they are not doing you any favors.

Female lifters encounter two major difficulties. First, almost all exercises and programs are tailored to male lifters. Second, female lifters have difficulty finding competition. Even in states with more than 100 lifters at their state championship meets, there will only be 6 to 10 women distributed across several weight classes. Also, they are not usually taken seriously as strength athletes, which discourages most women from participating in the sport.

Commitment and personal life are very important in this sport. In some sports, such as swimming or gymnastics, the top competitors are in their teens or early twenties and still living with their parents. In powerlifting, most athletes are well into their thirties when they achieve national prominence. It is in these years that the obligations of work and family life also become demanding. Without a strong commitment and strong support from family and friends, many potentially great lifters drop out of the sport.

Beginners search for the one perfect program and quickly learn that there is not one program but many different programs that accomplish the same things. Many beginners will switch training programs often on the advice of their training partners, other powerlifters in the gym, or articles in powerlifting magazines. Sometimes beginners will switch to the program used by the person who beat them in the last meet. After several training cycles and competitions, beginners will learn what works best for them and be able to develop a training program that produces the best results. All people are different and need to make adjustments that will fit their needs.

This chapter offers training programs for the squat, bench press, and deadlift. These programs are basic programs to start with and, if followed, they will increase strength. However, you don't want to just gain strength, you want to gain strength the fastest and most efficient way possible. Therefore, you are encouraged to continue learning and experimenting with your program in order to develop the ideal program for you. Lifters who compete usually train in the order of meet competition: squat, bench press, and deadlift. Some people perform the squat and deadlift once a week and others perform them every 10 days. These sessions are spaced so that every three to five days they are performing either a squat or deadlift. The reason for this is that both exercises use the same muscles and both are very strenuous exercises that require at least three days of recovery. The bench press is usually performed two times each week, three days apart, and includes a heavy day and a light day.

Squat Training Program

The squat is the most difficult of the three lifts to learn properly. Bar placement, foot placement, hand placement, body positioning, breathing, use of the belt, and strokes (the down and up movements) all have to be learned properly or you will never become a great squatter. You should make a habit of practicing proper techniques during every training session. It is an advantage to have a knowledgeable training partner who will constantly remind you of the proper techniques and instantly correct you if you do the exercise incorrectly.

A beginner should remember that the amount of weight lifted is not as important as proper techniques. Once you have mastered the proper techniques, you will find the amount of weight you are able to lift will increase rapidly. Proper technique also reduces the possibility of injuries.

This program consists of a light, medium, and heavy phase with a "max out" at the end of the heavy phase. The time for each phase is (1) five weeks of a light phase, consisting of 3 sets of 8 reps; (2) three weeks of a medium phase, consisting of 3 sets of 5 reps; and (3) two weeks of a heavy phase, consisting of 3 sets of 2 or 3 reps.

Light Phase

This phase begins with 1 or 2 sets of 10 to 12 reps for a warm-up. This weight should be approximately 50% of your maximum. During your warm-ups, ask your partner to correct you on the spot if you make a mistake, especially in the depth of your lift. This is the time to find your feel for the correct technique and should be carried over into your workout reps.

After the warm-up, proceed to your workout weight, which should be a weight that you can lift eight times with the last lift requiring a total effort on your part, which is near failure or failure. Remember to always have a competent spotter while squatting. During any part of this cycle, if you can do additional reps, you should add weight. If you train with a weight that is too light, you will not gain strength and muscle at the fastest possible rate.

Example (Assuming your max is 200 pounds)

2 × 100 × 12 (2 sets lifting 100 pounds doing 12 reps)

3 × 125 × 8 (3 sets lifting 125 pounds doing 8 reps)

Support Work

Support work is used to strengthen muscles in areas that are not getting enough stimulation during the squat. Examples of these muscles are the quadriceps (front of leg), hamstrings (back of leg), adductors (inner leg, or groin), abductors (outer leg), and calves (lower leg). You should use a weight that you can lift for 3 sets of 8 after doing a warm-up.

Medium Phase

The medium phase also starts with a good warm-up before proceeding to the workout weight. This phase sometimes requires a transition set or a set somewhere between your warm-up and workout weight but no more than 1 to 3 reps.

The workout weight is a weight you can lift five times, reaching near failure, or failure on the last rep each time.

Example (Assuming a 200-pound max)

2 × 100 × 12

1 × 125 × 3 to 5

3 × 150 × 5

Support Work

You should continue your support work during this phase. The amount of weight should increase in proportion to the increase in your workout weight (10%, 15%), and the reps should be reduced to match your workout reps.

Heavy Phase

The heavy phase also starts with a warm-up phase and possibly two transition phases of 1 rep each before proceeding to the workout weight.

The workout weight is a weight you can lift two or three times, reaching near failure or failure on the last rep of each set.

Example (Assuming a 200-pound max)

$2 \times 100 \times 12$ $1 \times 175 \times 1$

$1 \times 140 \times 1$ $3 \times 195 \times 2$ or 3

Support Work

Support work should not be done during this phase because of the intensity of the workout. However, if you want to continue doing support work, use lighter weights with 5 to 8 reps.

Max Out or Competition

At this point of the cycle, you should either be entering a competition or testing yourself by doing the maximum amount of weight you are capable of, to determine how much strength you have gained. Either way that you decide to test yourself will be a good indicator of your improvements. Take about one week off and start again in the light phase and continue doing cycles until you have reached your goals.

Bench Press Training Program

The main muscles to develop for a good bench press are the chest (pectorals) and back of arms (triceps). However, there are other muscles that are extremely important to an elite bench presser. The anterior deltoids (front of shoulders), serratus anteriors (on each side between the shoulders and waist), and latissimus dorsi (big muscle in upper and middle back) contribute to a good bench press. You should also have good flexibility in the lower back and hip area (front and back) in order to have a good arch while pressing.

Light Phase

Example (Assuming a 150-pound max)

$1 \times$ bar $\times 12$ $1 \times 95 \times 8$

$1 \times 85 \times 8$ $1 \times 75 \times 8$

$3 \times 105 \times 8$

Support Work

Refer to pages 116 through 129 for instructions and illustrations of these exercises.

Pressdown on lat bar (triceps)—3 sets of 8

Nose breakers (triceps)—3 sets of 8

Dumbbell flys (pectorals)—3 sets of 8

Front dumbbell raises (anterior deltoids)—3 sets of 8

Wide bench press (serratus anterior)—3 sets of 8

Medium Phase

Example

$1 \times$ bar $\times 12$ $1 \times 105 \times 8$

$1 \times 95 \times 8$ $1 \times 85 \times 8$

$3 \times 125 \times 8$ (if you can do more, move up to 130)

Support Work

Do support exercises the same as the light phase, but increase the weight at least 10%.

Heavy Phase

Example

$1 \times$ bar $\times 12$ $1 \times 125 \times 5$

$1 \times 105 \times 3$ $1 \times 105 \times 5$

3×140 or 145×2 or 3

Support Work

Due to the intensity of the heavy phase, you should not perform support work.

Deadlift Training Program

The deadlift is a total-body, functional exercise. *Functional* means that the techniques learned doing this movement are the same as for lifting anything from the floor, including bags of groceries, boxes of books, and small children without injuring your back. Once you have mastered the fundamentals and perfected the techniques, the amount of weight you can lift will amaze you. This is an easier lift than the squat, and you can usually lift more weight using the deadlift than the squat.

Light Phase

Example (Assuming a 200-pound max)

$2 \times 100 \times 10$

$3 \times 125 \times 8$

Support Work

See pages 116 through 129 for exercise instructions.

Leg press—$3 \times 120 \times 8$

Lunges—$3 \times BW \times 10$ body weight only

Good mornings—$3 \times 45 \times 10$

Medium Phase

This phase also starts with a good warm-up before proceeding to the workout weight. This phase sometimes requires a transition set or a set somewhere between your warm-up and workout weight, but it is no more than 1 to 3 reps.

Example (Assuming a 200-pound max)

$2 \times 100 \times 12$

$1 \times 125 \times 3$ to 5

$3 \times 150 \times 5$

Support Work

You should continue your support work during this phase. The amount of weight should increase in proportion to the increase in your workout weight (10%, 15%) and the reps should be reduced to match your workout reps.

Heavy phase

The heavy phase also starts with a warm-up phase and possibly two transition phases of 1 rep each before proceeding to the workout weight. The workout weight is a weight you can lift 2 or 3 times, reaching near failure or failure on the last rep of each set.

Example (Assuming a 200-pound max)

2 × 100 × 12	1 × 175 × 1
1 × 140 × 1	3 × 195 × 2 or 3

After finishing this cycle, you should either enter a competitive meet or take a week off and start the cycle again. The new cycle will involve increasing the weight in each phase. If you are entering a competitive meet, you should take at least five to seven days of rest before the day of the meet. This will allow the body to recover from the heavy phase of the cycle with full stores of energy.

Each cycle should be carefully documented in your notebook and your next cycle should be planned using information from your last cycle. After a year of cycling, go back and look at your first cycle. You will be amazed at what you have accomplished. Be patient and stick with your program; it will work.

Training for Other Sports

Some exercises are more useful than others for different sports. Knowing how to select the proper exercises for your sport is difficult at first, but it becomes easy with practice. You must determine

1. what movements are most important in the sport,
2. what muscles perform these movements, and
3. what exercises produce strength in those muscles.

With these guidelines in mind, you can determine what type of program works best for you. Following are two examples of how to select the proper exercises for a sport.

Football Lineman

The duty of the lineman is to stop or run over the opposing lineman to protect a quarterback or sack a quarterback. The lineman uses the four-point stance (hands and feet on ground) and at the start of the play he is to lunge forward against another player, using the

An athlete whose sport requires an explosive burst of energy can benefit from powerlifting exercises and techniques.

power of his legs, hips, lower back, and gluteal muscles. The lineman also uses the upper body, especially the arms, shoulders, and chest muscles, to push away or tackle another player. Now that we have established that the lower and upper body are both important, we can begin to select appropriate exercises.

For the Lower Body

Squats—to strengthen the legs, hips, and lower back for the powerful lunge forward.

Leg extension—to strengthen the quadriceps, to increase padding for protection of the leg bones, and to stabilize the knees.

The football player uses the muscles of the upper and lower body, especially when lunging forward to tackle another player.

Leg flexion (curls)—to strengthen the hamstrings and to stabilize the knees.

Lunges—to strengthen the hip and leg muscles.

Leg press or sled—to strengthen the hip and leg muscles.

Heel raises (seated and standing)—to strengthen the calf muscles for stabilizing the ankles.

For the Upper Body

Bench press—to strengthen the chest muscles for pushing and to increase padding for protection of the chest area.

Seated or bent-over row—to strengthen the upper back for strength and padding for protection of the ribs.

Shoulder press—to strengthen and pad the shoulder area, which is used to hit or push.

Lat pull—to strengthen the muscles of the middle and upper back for protection.

Biceps curl—to develop pulling and holding strength and to stabilize the elbows.

Triceps extension—to develop pushing strength and to stabilize the elbows during contact.

Basketball Player

The basketball player is generally much taller than other athletes. Although height is an advantage in basketball, it can be a handicap as far as injuries are concerned. Longer limbs are more susceptible to injuries in the knees, ankles, and hips. Therefore, the basketball player needs to do strenuous strength training to protect the joints, muscles, and bones of the lower body. The basketball player's duties are to shoot, pass, dribble, make fast starts and fast stops, and execute high jumps and quick lateral moves. He or she must be big enough and strong enough to establish and hold a position under the basket. A quick analysis of these moves quickly shows us that every muscle in the body is important in basketball.

For the Lower Body

Squats—to strengthen the hips, quadriceps, and hamstrings, which strengthen and stabilize the knees to produce starts, stops, and jumps.

Lunges—same as the squat.

A basketball player must have overall strength in order to hold positions under the basket.

Leg extension—to strengthen the quadriceps.

Leg flexion (curl)—to strengthen hamstrings.

Heel raises—to strengthen calf muscles to stabilize the ankles.

Leg press or sled—same as the squat.

For the Upper Body

Bench Press—to strengthen the chest, front of the shoulder, and triceps.

Bent-over or seated row—to strengthen the upper back.

Shoulder press—to strengthen the middle and posterior shoulder muscles. Basketball players have well-developed shoulder muscles, which come from thrusting their arms upward while jumping.

Triceps pressdowns—to strengthen the triceps for shooting and to stabilize the elbows.

Biceps curls—to stabilize the elbows.

Summary

You have learned how to carefully plan a training program that leads to the goal of ultimate strength. You now know that you must set a goal and work toward that goal using scientific knowledge, dedication, patience, proper training, proper nutrition, and proper rest. These principles can be used to develop a program for any sport, not just powerlifting. Start a program and stick to it. Don't jump from one type of workout to another just because someone else is doing it. Believe in your program and believe in yourself.

CALF (SITTING)

The sitting calf exercise strengthens the soleus muscle, which is located under the gastrocnemius. The soleus muscle is used when the legs are flexed in a 90-degree position and the heels are raised and lowered, as in this exercise. Use a specially-designed machine that allows you to sit with the pad placed across the knees with the balls of the feet on a stationary pedal. Lower the heels as far as possible to achieve a stretch, then lift them as high as possible for a maximal contraction.

CALF (STANDING)

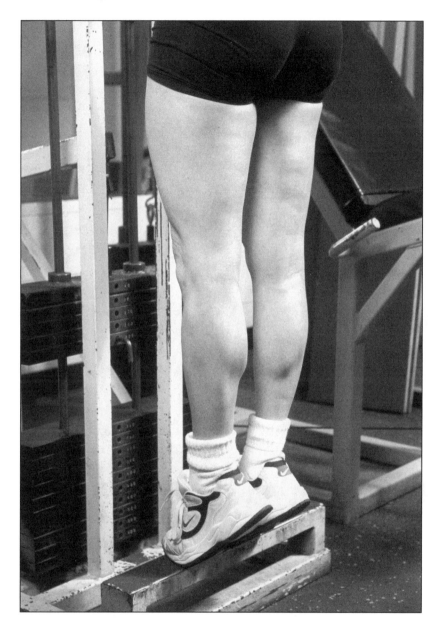

The standing calf exercise benefits the gastrocnemius muscle, or the outer muscle visible in the lower leg. The gastrocnemius muscle is used when the legs are straight, with knees not bent. This exercise can be done almost anywhere, either on both legs at once or one leg at a time. Any elevated step or bench will work as long as it is sturdy and stable. Place the balls of the feet on the step or bench. Lower the heels as far as possible to stretch the muscles, and then raise the heels as high as possible to achieve a maximal contraction. Try progressing from both legs to one leg and then to using hand-held weights.

DUMBBELL FLY

The dumbbell fly strengthens the pectoral muscles. Get into the bench press position, and hold a pair of dumbbells with the palms facing in an up position. The elbows should be bent slightly to create the "bowlegged" position that is held throughout the movement. Lower the weights slowly until you feel a stretch in the pectoral muscles, and then slowly return to the start position.

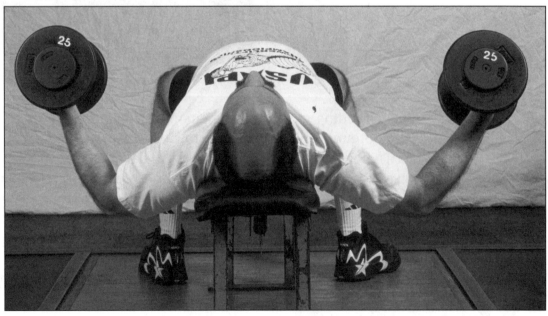

DUMBBELL PRESS

The dumbbell press is a variation of the bench press using dumbbells. This exercise allows the lifter to get an extra stretch in the pectoral area in the down position, and to determine if one arm is lazy and lags behind the other. Take the weights in an up position with the elbows locked out. The thumbs should be facing, as if you are holding a bar. Lower the weights, as if you were lowering a bar, and then press back to the start position.

FRONT DUMBBELL RAISE

 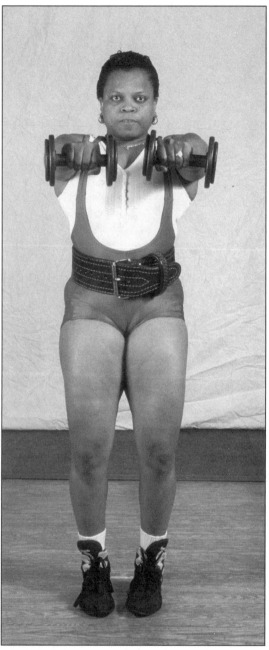

The front dumbbell raise strengthens the anterior deltoids (front of the shoulder). Hold a dumbbell in each hand with the knuckles up and the palms facing the body. From this position, lift straight up without bending the elbows until the arms are horizontal to the floor, then slowly lower the arms to the start position.

GOOD MORNINGS

The good morning exercise benefits advanced lifters who are already in good physical condition but are trying to isolate the hamstring, gluteal, and lower-back muscles. The bar is placed on the back in a high bar position near the base of the neck. Spread your feet to shoulder width and slightly flex the knees. Keeping the head up, bend forward until the torso is horizontal with the floor, then slowly return to the start position. The first time you perform this exercise, try starting with only the bar and then add weight slowly over the next several sessions until you have a good idea of what you can lift without injury.

HAMSTRING FLEXION

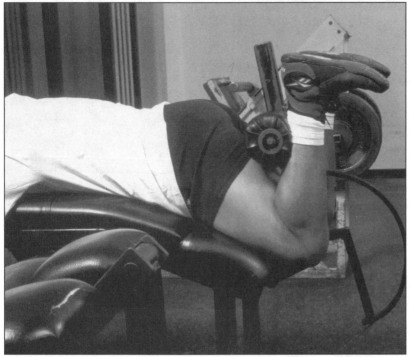

The hamstrings are the large muscles on the back of the upper leg. One of their primary purposes is to flex the knee. In this exercise, lie face down and place your heels behind the roller pad. Flex the legs by bringing the heels as close to the buttocks as possible, then slowly return to the start position.

LUNGE

The lunge is one of the easiest and most effective exercises for the muscles from the waist down. Start in a standing position with feet together. Take a step forward with either leg, far enough that when the lead leg is bent to a 90-degree flexion the knee is directly over the foot. Push the back leg down but do not allow it to touch the floor. From this position, push back with the lead leg to the start position. Hand-held weights (dumbbells) can be used when you are ready to increase the resistance beyond body weight.

NARROW GRIP BENCH PRESS

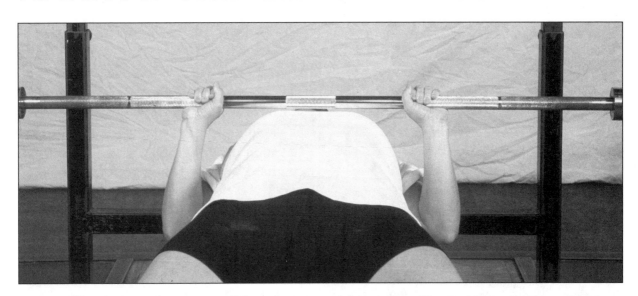

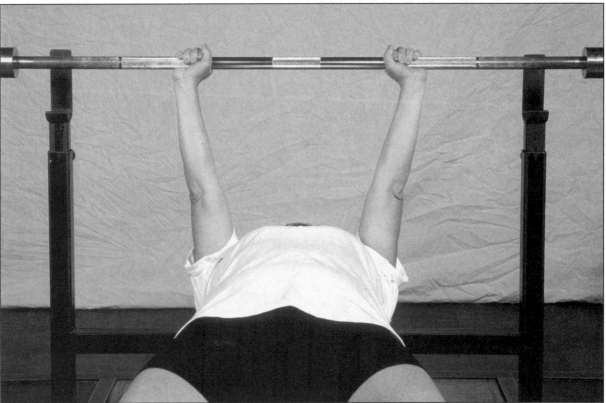

The narrow grip bench press places added stress on the triceps muscles. Start in the same position as the regular bench press with the exception of the hand width. Place the hands in a narrower than normal position and do regular bench press motions. Experiment with the width of the hands, placing them as close together as you can without causing wrist pain. A spotter is a must.

NOSE BREAKER

The nose breaker places extra stress on the triceps muscles. Use the same position on the bench as the regular bench press. The exercise is usually done with a curved bar, but you can substitute a straight bar also. When your spotter hands you the bar, take it in a locked elbow position with the hands about 8 inches apart. Lower the bar slowly toward the nose while keeping the elbows pointed straight up. When the bar is approximately 1 inch from the nose, push back to a straight arm position without changing the position of the elbows. The spotter's hand should be positioned so that he or she can catch the bar before it hits the lifter in the face.

PRESS DOWN ON LAT BAR

This is a triceps exercise using the latissimus dorsi bar. Take a comfortable position and grasp the bar with the hands close together and the elbows pressed tightly against the ribs at the sides. Press down until you touch your thighs, then slowly return to the start position. Do not allow your elbows to move away from your ribs, and make sure there is no movement of the torso.

QUADRICEPS EXTENSION

The quadriceps are the large muscles on the front of the upper leg. One of their purposes is to extend the knee. Sit in the chair part of the machine and place your feet behind the roller pads. Straighten the legs with a slow and steady movement until you achieve full contraction, then slowly lower the legs to the start position.

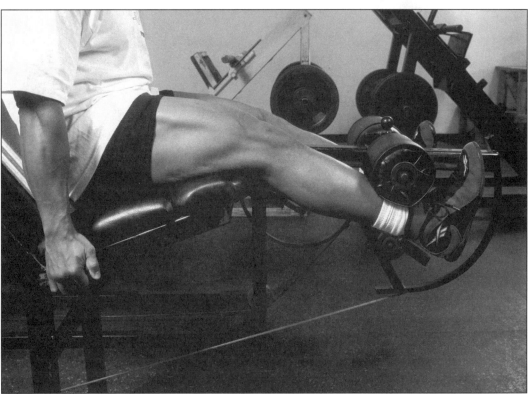

SLED

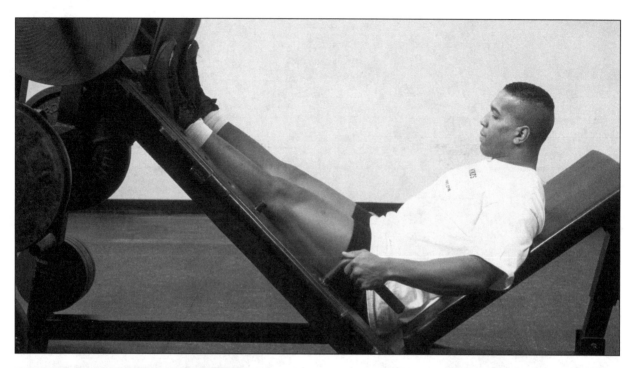

The sled exercise simulates the squat move and develops the same muscles. All of the muscles from the waist down are used in some way in this exercise. Lie on your back and place your feet on the pedal. Spread the feet to shoulder width with the toes turned slightly outward. Allow the pedal to slowly push the legs back until the knees are at a 90-degree angle, and then slowly push to a straight leg position without locking the knees.

WIDE GRIP BENCH PRESS

The wide grip bench press develops the pectoral muscles by placing added stress on them. This exercise starts in the same position as the regular bench press with the exception of the width between the hands. Place your hands farther apart than normal and then do the regular bench press movements. Experiment with the width of your hands, placing them as far apart as you can without causing pain in the wrist. Be sure you have a good spotter while doing this exercise.

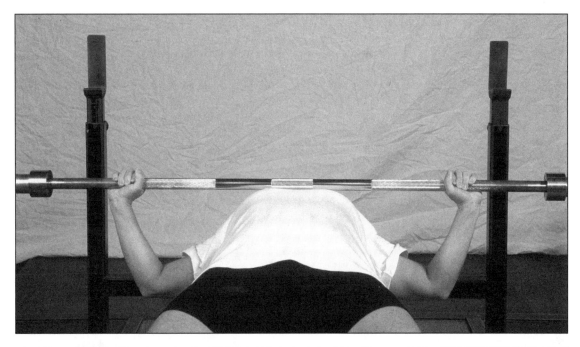

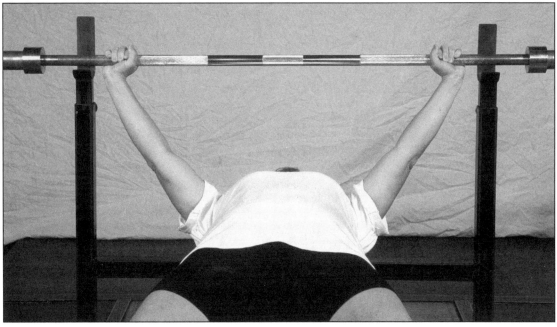

Psyched to Lift

9

What is this thing called "psyching up"? Is it real or a myth? It *is* real and dates back to the beginning of humankind. My apologies to the purist who reads this book, because I've taken some liberties in telling the story in a more interesting and simplified manner. In his book *The Wisdom of the Body* (NY: W.W. Norton, 1932), Walter B. Cannon discusses a theory he developed that for many years has proven to be true and can be put to use in a positive way. Cannon developed the "fight or flight" theory, which is based on another theory that a very important physiological change took place during the caveman days: the development of the adrenal gland. The adrenal gland produces adrenaline, which when injected into the bloodstream gives a person a boost of energy. For example, imagine yourself as a caveman, walking along with your trusty club. You come face to face with a saber-toothed tiger. You have a choice at this point: either fight the tiger, or try to outrun the tiger—fight or flee. It is believed that those who survived these situations had a physiological component that enabled them to gear up for some fast action, and they passed this ability along to their children, creating a race of winners and survivors. Those that did not possess this ability either became tiger bait or a cave potato and didn't survive the cut, because now everyone has an adrenal gland.

Adrenaline produces maximum effort from the muscles and produces feats of strength that are much greater than anyone ever thought possible. So the secret to great strength is the ability to control the adrenal gland and cause it to produce adrenaline at the time it is desired. How can you cause the adrenal gland to produce adrenaline? Extreme fear, anger, and happiness can cause the gland to "kick start" your physiological motor. Therefore, you must develop a way to simulate one of these adrenaline-producing emotions. You must use the power of your mind and the power of your muscles as a team to produce the greatest results.

The mind plays a very important role in strength. It can keep you from making a lift if you are in a negative mode, but if your mind is in a positive mode, it can cause you to lift more weight than you ever thought possible. Achieving this positive mental mode is complicated and will require a lot of practice. You must learn how to make your mind work for you in order to increase your lifting ability. The mind reaches a psychological limit before the body reaches a physiological limit, which means that our mind tells our muscles to quit before reaching their true limit. This is a safety feature the body uses to protect the muscles from being injured. However, injury is not a problem in well-conditioned muscles if you use proper technique. Therefore, pushing for 100% will not injure a lifter except in rare cases. Torn pectoral (chest) muscles, pulled biceps muscles, and damaged tendons or cartilage in the knees happen only under extreme conditions using very heavy weights in high-level competition. We have been programmed from an early age to strain ourselves to a point that is less than 100%. However, if we want to compete, we need to learn how to exert 100% of our strength during training and competition.

Have you ever wondered why two men the same size have such different lifting abilities? One man says to himself, "I know I can do it," while the other man says, "I don't think I can do it." If you have a negative attitude, you might as well go home and become the world's best couch potato, because you will never be a winner. Why is it that some smaller people can lift more than larger people? The reason is that small people live in a world designed for bigger people, and small people must adjust for the differences. One of the most important adjustments small people have to make is in the area of strength. Heavy doors, bags of groceries, and spare tires have no ability to change weight according to the size of the person handling these things.

Can you program yourself to become stronger by putting more effort into each workout and in turn receiving more benefits from each workout? Yes, you can determine the quality of your workouts and your performance during competitions. How can you tap into all of your abilities while training and competing?

I have observed some bizarre and unhealthy methods of psyching up for a lift. I have seen lifters hit themselves in the forehead with a two-by-four piece of wood, butt the squat bar with their forehead, and have another person slap their face, hit them on the back, or say insulting things to them. Some lifters have developed elaborate rituals that they repeat before each lift. These rituals include sniffing ammonia, yelling, repeating a chant, and walking a certain way when approaching the bar.

Bill Kazmaier, one of the world's best-known strongmen, imagines tragic things happening to his family and takes his anger out on the weights. Two high school boys in Texas use "rancor lifting" or "hate lifting" and have achieved good results. They look for things that make them mad and remember each of these things to take their anger out on the weights. Personally, I would never injure myself to psych up for a lift, nor would I advise it for others. There are other ways of psyching up without injury. The other methods, such as rituals or other tricks with the imagination, seem to be healthy ways of preparing for the lift. If it works, stay with it.

Until recently, all but a few lifters had overlooked the use of mental skills to improve physical skills. Most professional and collegiate teams employ sport psychologists. Many world-class and Olympic competitors have psychologists on their team of trainers. Psychological techniques include mental imagery, meditation, and hypnosis. The mind is a powerful tool and knowing how to use your mind in a positive way can make a difference in your life, whether you are a winner or just another competitor.

Mental Imagery

An athlete uses mental imagery to simulate reality by mentally rehearsing a movement, imagining visual (seeing), auditory (hearing), kinesthetic (feeling), olfactory (smelling), and physical movement cues. Dwight Stone, an Olympic high jumper, mentally practiced his jump in his mind. While he prepared to jump, he went through every step, turn, and movement in his mind several times before actually performing the jump. Jack Nicklaus, a world-famous golfer, says that he visualizes the flight and landing of the ball before every shot.

In order to learn any skill, you should start simple and practice until you can move on to the complicated movements or series of complicated movements. For example, imagine a bar on a squat rack. Then imagine yourself getting under the bar and adjusting the bar to the position on your back. Now, stand straight up with the weight on your back. Back out, first step, second step. Make additional foot adjustments, then straighten up and look at the head judge. The head judge gives you the command to squat. You then take a deep breath, push your abdomen against the belt, and tighten your muscles as you begin your descent. Upon reaching parallel, you thrust your head back while pushing hard against the floor to begin your ascent. Then you push the buttocks through as you straighten your knees for a lockout. Are you able to do as suggested? You are probably thinking, This is easy. But did you really feel the bar, could you see a head judge, did you smell the baby powder and liniment, did your heart rate increase, and did you feel yourself begin to pump adrenaline into your bloodstream? When you can do all of this for every movement and really feel your body preparing for the lift, then you are successful in using imagery.

Meditation

Meditation is the art of focusing. To meditate effectively, you must find a quiet place and clear your mind of everything except what you are about to do. Don't let anything or anyone else, except during an emergency, become part of your focus. Maintain your focus until the workout is over and then spend another few minutes returning to the real world. This practice feels like a waste of time at first. But when you learn to use it effectively, you wouldn't consider doing a workout or participating in a meet until you have had this clearing of the mind.

Hypnosis

Hypnosis is the ability to be convinced either by another person or yourself, through suggestions, that you have the ability or potential to achieve a certain goal. Hypnosis can be defined as a state of sleep or trance induced in a person by means of verbal suggestion by a hypnotist or by concentration on an object. A powerlifter concentrates on an object in order to achieve the effects of a *hypnotic trance*. Although the person is not actually in a trance, he or she appears to be because of the ability to focus totally on the lift. The lifter concentrates all energy, both mind and body, on one task, allowing himself or herself to give 100%. Hypnosis cannot give you additional strength, endurance, or skill, but it can release your inhibitions and allow you to use the abilities you already have.

If you are already performing 100% of your potential, hypnosis will not improve your performance. However, if you have trouble giving 100%, you need to develop the ability to block out everything but the task at hand and focus on the lift. If this is not developed, you might be wondering about the next lift, the pretty girl in the front row, or where you will go out to eat tonight, and miss the lift. You can block out everything around you with practice, but you must practice this during your training and not wait until the meet. However, don't think for one second that this type of thing can replace a hard workout. It will not, and you should only use it to increase the quality and intensity of your workouts. Also, only a small portion of the population can achieve the effective state of mind known as the hypnotic trance, so don't worry if this procedure does not work immediately for you.

Priorities

Establish your priorities and stick to them. I remember when I first began to compete and would be working out, or on my way to a workout, and someone would begin to ask questions and engage me in conversation, which would divert me from what I was trying to do. Students would appear at my door just as I was leaving to work out and want "only five minutes of my time" to ask a question about a class, even though they knew I had designated office hours. They would also come to the weight room and begin to ask questions while I was working out. This was also true of other faculty members who did not share my values about working out. After a while, I realized I would never be able to do high-quality workouts until I established some rules about my time. I schedule 90 minutes a day to work out without interruption and stick to it, barring an emergency. I try not to be rude but I stick to my plan and politely but firmly tell intruders that I will be back in my office at a certain time.

Summary

You have learned the importance of using the abilities of the mind to improve the abilities of the body. These abilities include

1. learning to get the adrenaline rush that provides the physiological boost for an all-out effort,

2. learning to focus on the task at hand by using imagery, meditation, and self-hypnosis, and

3. learning to value your time in the weight room and demand that it be respected by others.

All of these methods aid in the improvement of workouts and competition; they are not meant to take the place of any physical training efforts.

Competition

10

If you are a beginning lifter and have been working out and showing progress, you are wondering, "How good am I?" "Am I good enough to compete?" "Would I make a fool of myself?" "Will the other lifters make fun of me?" The only way to really know the answers to all of these questions is to start competing. I remember my first meet and how anxious and nervous I was. I was 55 years old, and I still went through all the anxieties that a young person experiences. During my years of competition, no other lifter has ever made me feel bad. Powerlifters are very supportive of other lifters (even if they are opponents) through encouraging words, helping with gear, and cheering during a lift.

So, you have decided you want to enter a meet and compete. Now what? How do you find out where the next meet will be, the time of the meet, the cost of entering, and what happens after arriving at the meet?

Powerlifting meets are not well publicized and establishing yourself in the first meet is very difficult. Following are some suggestions on how to become a part of the powerlifting society.

How to Find a Meet to Enter

If you have been working out at a gym that has powerlifters, you probably already know how to enter a meet. Buy a powerlifting magazine, published monthly in most cases, that has a list of the meets scheduled throughout the country. These listings range from a local high school meet to a national or world-class meet. The listings will give the address, date, time, and phone number of the meet director. You can write or call the meet director to request registration forms and any additional information they send out. The forms usually have information concerning the categories of lifters (for example, open, submasters, masters, juniors). They will list the weight categories from the 123-pound weight class to the super heavyweight class. They will also tell you how many trophies will be awarded in each weight class.

Another way is to call or visit a gym or fitness facility and ask if they have information concerning powerlifting meets. Usually the gyms that cater to serious weightlifters will have the information you want. Fitness centers don't consider competition necessary to stay physically fit, but meet directors might send information to them anyway.

How to Enter in the Proper Category

Powerlifting competition is divided into several different categories, with age, gender, and body weight as the factors used to determine categories. This arrangement puts each lifter in a class of people with similar age and weight. Find the category that fits your age and weight, and register for that. You must meet the weight requirement, which is determined by a weigh-in on the evening before the day of the meet, or if you intend to set a new record you must weigh in on the day of the meet.

Rules Meeting

The meet director will have a meeting each day to discuss the rules, usually immediately before lifting begins. It is a good idea to attend the meeting even if you have a rulebook. During this meeting the general rules will be discussed as well as some specific rules pertaining to this meet. I have been to many rules meetings over the years and still learn something each time I attend. I would highly recommend attending each meeting.

Warm-Up Room

The warm-up room was very intimidating the first few times I attended meets. I would go into a room that was full of big, muscular people and try to concentrate on warming up. I was unsure of the protocol for using a bar, and I didn't want to infringe on anyone, but I needed to do my warm-up. I soon discovered that a little effort to communicate with the people around me took all the stress out of the situation because other people had the same anxieties I did. All the powerlifters I have met are very courteous, polite, helpful, and friendly people. I guess if you are around that many really strong

Concentration and strategy are important factors in a good powerlifting competition.

people, a bad temper could be hazardous to your health. Make friends, because you will continue to see many of the same people from meet to meet.

Lifting Gear

Some gear is used in all lifts. However, not all lifters use equipment the same way and think that other equipment is not necessary. For squat lifts, almost every lifter wears a squat suit, knee wraps, and a lifting belt. After a few competitions a lifter will usually add squat shoes and wrist wraps.

A bench presser will wear wrist wraps, bench press shirt, and a belt. A belt is not standard for a bench presser, but some do use them.

Almost all deadlifters wear a belt as standard equipment. Advanced lifters will also wear a specially constructed body suit. The suit is designed to help a lifter straighten up by giving support to the back. Most lifters also wear special shoes. These are flat-soled shoes resembling wrestling shoes or bedroom slippers. Do not wear shoes with thick soles—you do *not* want extra height to start lifting the bar.

Timing

Knowing what to wear is important but knowing when to put the gear on is also very important. The most commonly used equipment and gear is described in detail in chapter 7. Here we discuss the importance of timing when to suit up during a meet.

Usually after the rules meeting, the lifters are given 30 minutes to warm up to start the first flight if there are enough lifters for more than one flight. If you are in the first flight, you need to quickly put on your squat suit and start warming up to prepare for your first lift. Also, check to determine where you are placed within the flight. If you are first, you need to hustle, but if you are last, lie back a little and time your last warm-up lift with your first competition lift.

Squat Suit

The squat suit that fits tight enough to give maximum support will take about 20 minutes to put on. This is usually with the help of at least one partner and preferably two. This piece of gear is very uncomfortable and should not be worn longer than necessary.

Knee Wraps

Knee wraps for the squat are very painful if properly applied and should not be worn longer than necessary. It is ideal to have an experienced person wrap your knees for you, but that is not always possible, so learn to do it yourself. The announcer will call the name of the lifter, the next lifter (on deck), and you (in the hole). Watch for the person lifting to get under the bar and then begin to wrap your knees. This should give you plenty of time to wrap, get your straps up, tighten your belt, and put on your wrist wraps to be ready for your turn. You have one minute from the time "the bar is loaded" command is given by the head judge to receive your signal to squat. Take enough time to set up properly, but don't delay unnecessarily; you are using valuable energy.

Belt

The lifting belt is the most common piece of equipment for weightlifters. It is a valuable tool to support the back by reinforcing the abdominal muscles. It takes a while to learn how to get the most help from a belt. The belt should be tight enough to give abdominal support, but not so tight that it interferes with breathing. A tightened belt greatly raises the blood pressure, so tighten it at the last moment before the lift and loosen it as quickly as possible after the lift.

Wrist Wraps

Wrist wraps are usually not worn tight enough to be painful or uncomfortable and should be the first thing to go on and the last thing to come off. Always remember to take the thumb loops off after wrapping, because it is against the rules to leave them on during competition.

Bench Press Shirt

The bench press shirt is another very uncomfortable piece of gear. If properly fitted, it will take at least one other person, preferably two, to put it on you. You should carefully time when you will put the shirt on so that you will wear it the shortest possible length of time. The arms are forced forward and up, so it is most comfortable to have something or someone support the arms to keep them level with the shoulders. As miserable as it is to put on and wear, it adds to the amount of weight you can lift and protects against shoulder injuries.

Deadlift Suit

The deadlift suit is another very uncomfortable piece of gear, especially for men. This suit is a relatively new piece of equipment used by lifters. The fabric runs up and down the body, as opposed to horizontally around the body as the squat suit does. This fabric, along with the way the suit is constructed, pulls the lifter into an upright position making it difficult to bend over and grasp the bar. The suit then aids the lifter in the initial pull from the floor all the way through to the finish position.

Deadlift Shoes

Deadlift shoes are usually slippers; some lifters wear actual bedroom slippers. Sometimes flat-soled shoes, similar to wrestling shoes with as little elevation as possible, are worn. The soles should be made of a nonslip material. These are not very comfortable to walk around in because of a lack of cushioning for the feet.

Meet Strategy

It is very important to have a strategy going into a meet. You will be much more relaxed and able to focus if you have a plan and know what weights you are going to use, at least for the opening lift. You may change your original plan as you go along, but it does help to be prepared.

Opening Weights

When you weigh in before competing, you will be asked to supply your opening weights on all three lifts. You must remember that if you don't successfully make your opening lift with the weight you listed you cannot go to a lower weight. If you try and fail three times you are out of the meet (bombed out) from that point on. Therefore, it is very important that you open with a weight you can handle in good form. Lifters have different strategies for determining this beginning weight. Some will open with the weight that they doubled or tripled during their last week of training and some will open with even less. The idea is to do the first lift in perfect form, going deep to impress the judges.

Experienced lifters will tell you to "get in the meet" first and then try for the records. To bomb out is a bad experience, especially if it is the squat that is always at the beginning of the meet.

Your plans for the meet should have been made by the last workout. Don't go to the meet wondering what to open with and while there begin to have doubts. If this happens you might as well turn around and go home, because if you wonder if you can make the lift, you won't.

Second Lift

Your second lift should be based on how you felt during the first lift. If it felt easy, then go for a personal record (PR), but if it was heavy, make a small increase and go for the PR on the third lift.

Third Lift

Your third lift could be the most important decision you make during the meet. For example, if you are in close competition with another lifter for first place, you cannot afford to take a chance on missing your third lift and giving up valuable points. However, if you are so far ahead or so far behind that it doesn't matter, then that is the time to go for it.

Advice

Advice is plentiful; everyone has some they want to give away. The only person you take advice from at a meet is your coach, or if you don't have a coach, listen to your training partner. These people know you and your capabilities and will help you make the right decisions. Don't make enemies, but don't take advice from everyone willing to give it to you.

Summary

This chapter gives you an idea of what happens from the time you sign up for a meet to when the last lift is over. You must make good decisions concerning what weight class you are trying be in, and about what weights to open with and how much to move up for your second and third attempts. You will likely ask yourself the following questions. Should I lose weight and get in a lower class or keep the weight and stay in a higher weight class? What assistive gear do I plan to use during the meet, when do I put it on, and who will help me put it on? When is the best time to start my warm-up, and how much should I do during warm-up? Do I just want to win the meet, or do I want to set a new state, regional, or national record? You will make a lot of mistakes while learning strategy, but you will gain useful experience from each one you make. Don't be discouraged if you are not immediately successful; it is the final outcome that is important, so have patience and never quit.

Locators followed by *f* indicate reference to figures; locators followed by *t* indicate reference to tables.

Barney Groves has been a weightlifter for more than four decades and a weight-training instructor at the university level for almost as long. As a certified strength and conditioning specialist, he has also been a strength coach and consultant for several college teams. He is the coauthor of two other weight-training books from Human Kinetics—the top-selling *Weight Training: Steps to Success* and its companion, *Weight Training Instruction: Steps to Success*.

Groves began powerlifting in 1991 at the age of 55, and since that time, he has set state, regional, and National records in the squat. He has competed in two to four meets each year, placing first in every meet but one. Currently, he is the Virginia state and regional champion for the 60 and older age group.

Groves holds a PhD in physical education from Florida State University and is a professor of physical education at Virginia Commonwealth University. He lives in New Kent, Virginia, with his wife, Patsy. When he's not lifting, Groves enjoys flying and working on his 113-acre farm.